Life After High School

Valuable Life Skills for the Goal-Oriented Achiever!

WORKBOOK

A Practical Workbook to Making Responsible
& Wise Adult Decisions

Dr. Mia Y. Merritt

Decisions, Decisions, & More Decisions!

Copyright © 2010
by Mia Y. Merritt, Ed.D
Life After High School Workbook:
Valuable Life Skills for the Goal-Oriented Achiever!

All rights reserved. No part of this book
may be reproduced in any form without permission
in writing from the author or publisher.

ISBN #978-0-9720398-7-1

Other Books by Mia Y. Merritt:
Prosperity is Your Birthright!
Prosperity is Your Birthright Workbook
Destined for Great Things!
Destined for Great Things Workbook
Words of Inspiration: Golden Nuggets for the Wise at Heart
Life After High School: Valuable Life Skills for the
Goal-Oriented Achiever!

Library of Congress Cataloging
in-Publication Data

Merritt, Mia

First Printing December 2011
Printed in the U.S.A.

Message From the Author: Dr. Mia Y. Merritt

As a result of this workbook, you will be able to write *meaningful* long and short term goals for your life, recognize your innate gifts, talents and skills, write down "how" you will prepare for your future through interview skills, resume writing, and job searches. Additionally, you will be able to write action plans for how you will maintain good credit and also how you will acquire wealth through implementing the financial "secrets" given to you from the book. This workbook is definitely a keeper and one to keep handy at all times!

Knowledge is power, but the application of knowledge is even more powerful. The most valuable lessons in life are learned through personal experiences and when you are able to look back and recognize the lessons learned from each of your experiences, you acquire wisdom. Life can sometimes be unpredictable, filled with so many uncertainties and sometimes curveballs, but if you already have the knowledge of common things to come, you will be in a better position to appropriately face and overcome those obstacles.

This practical, interactive, hands-on workbook was written to apply what you have learned from the book, *Life After High School, Valuable Life Skills for the Goal-Oriented Achiever!* It is one thing to read a book and remember some of the information from it, but when you can apply what you learned through written exercises and activities, you are more inclined to remember that information so that when you need it, it will be easily accessible at the forefront of your memory.

Kind Regards,

Dr. Mia Y. Merritt
President/CEO
M&M Motivating
www.miamerritt.com
1-866-560-7652

Goal-setting Quote:

The secret to productive goal setting is establishing clearly defined goals, writing them down and then focusing on them several times a day with words and emotions as if you've already achieved them.

Denis Waitley

Table of Contents

Message From the Author iii

Chapter 1: Why go to College 1

Chapter 2: Career Preparation 19

Chapter 3: Dating & Relationships 33

Chapter 4: Setting Goals & Strategic Planning 45

Chapter 5 Cultivating Your Gifts 53

Chapter 6: Your Credit Report 65

Chapter 7: Managing Your Money Strategically 75

Chapter 8: Sex, Diseases & Responsibilities 93

Chapter 9: Drugs & Alcohol.. 107

Chapter 10: Buying Your First Home 127

Chapter 11: All About the Military 145

Dr. Mia Y. Merritt, M&M Motivating
Life After High School: Valuable Life Skills for the Goal-Oriented Achiever!

This workbook belongs to:

_____

Date:

_____

1
Why go to College?

Two Cents worth:

You must strategically plan for your future.
Failing to plan is planning to fail.

Anonymous

DATE _____

1. On the lines below, write where you will be and what you plan on doing next year this time.

   _____

   _____

   _____

2. If you already know what college you want to attend, write the name of the college, whether it is a public or private college, and why you chose this particular university.

Name of College: _____

___ public   ___ private I am interesting in pursuing my degree at this particular college

because: _____

_____

_____

3. Name at least five benefits of going to college?

   I. _____

Dr. Mia Y. Merritt, M&M Motivating
Life After High School: Valuable Life Skills for the Goal-Oriented Achiever!

II. _____

III. _____

IV. _____

V. _____

4. What are some health advantages that college students have over non-college degree holders?

   I. _____

   II. _____

   III. _____

5. What is the difference between a public and a private college?

Private Colleges: _____

_____

_____

Public Colleges: _____

_____

_____

6. What are two ADVANTAGES of attending a public university?

   I. _____

   II. _____

7. What are two DISADVANTAGES of attending a public university?

   I. _____

II. _____

8. What are two ADVANTAGES of attending a private university?

   I. _____

   II. _____

9. What are two DISADVANTAGES of attending a private university?

   I. _____

   II. _____

10. How will your college education be paid for?

_____

_____

_____

11. What would you like to major in? _____

12. How will you choose your major?

_____

_____

_____

13. Why should you not go into college with an "undeclared" major?

_____

_____

_____

14. Name three things that your Academic Advisor does for you.

        I. _____

       II. _____

     III. _____

15. Do you know the number of courses you will need to take for the completion of your degree? ___ yes ___ no. If yes, how many? _____

16. How many classes would you like to take per semester? _____

17. Will you work while going to school? ___ yes ___ no. If yes, how many hours per week? _____. If yes, why do you have to work while in college? _____

_____

_____

_____

18. Based on your calculations, what will be your graduation month and year? _____

19. While pursuing your degree, what school will you be in? (school of business, school of communications, school of medicine, etc.) _____

20. What does academic probation mean? _____

_____

_____

21. What will you do to keep from getting on Academic Probation? _____

_____

_____

_____

22. What is a Financial Aid Packet? _____

Dr. Mia Y. Merritt, M&M Motivating
Life After High School: Valuable Life Skills for the Goal-Oriented Achiever!

_____

_____

23. What is a FAFSA and the importance of it?

_____

_____

_____

24. Name three advantages of living **on** campus.

    I. _____

    II. _____

    III. _____

25. Name three advantages of living **off** campus.

    I. _____

    II. _____

    III. _____

26. Name at least five of the fastest growing and highest paying jobs from the Department of Labor's forecast until 2014.

    I. _____

    II. _____

    III. _____

    IV. _____

    V. _____

27. Name at least five tips that you will apply while in college to make good grades.

    I. _____

    II. _____

    III. _____

    IV. _____

    V. _____

28. In your own words, what is the difference between the SAT and ACT?

SAT: _____

_____

_____

ACT: _____

_____

_____

29. What do BA and BS stand for?

    BA: _____

    BS: _____

30. What do AA and AS stand for?

    AA: _____

    AS: _____

31. What is the difference between BA/BS and AA/AS degrees?

_____

_____

_____

32. What is an internship? _____

_____

_____

33. Name at least four benefits that internships can do for you.

        I. _____

       II. _____

      III. _____

      IV. _____

34. Explain in your own words what a vocational/trade school is.

_____

_____

_____

35. What is the difference between a college and a vocational/trade school.

_____

_____

_____

36. What are some of the questions you should ask while seeking a good vocational/trade school?

        I. _____

       II. _____

      III. _____

      IV. _____

37. Name two benefits of attending a vocational/trade school.

       I. _____

      II. _____

TRUE/FALSE

38. Public schools are more expensive than private schools. _____

39. Each individual state has a public college that they regulate and fund. _____

40. If you do not maintain a certain G.P.A. for two consecutive semesters, a university can kick you out. _____

41. The college website tells you everything you need to know about the university. _____

42. All college internships are paid. _____

43. A perfect score on the ACT is 1600. _____

44. A perfect score on the SAT is 36. _____

45. Most college educated people have access to better healthcare. _____

46. Private colleges sometimes give you the incentive of name-recognition. _____

47. Some colleges will accept either the SAT or ACT scores. _____

48. If you don't graduate from college, you do not have to pay back the student loans. _____

49. A Bachelor's Degree normally requires 180 credits to graduate. _____

50. A "C" is an acceptable grade in college. _____

51. If you receive a "D" in a course, you do not have to take the course over. _____

52. If your GPA falls below a 2.5, you may get placed on academic probation. _____

53. Speaking and writing is the foundation of the college academic experience. _____

54. It is okay to party all night and then cram for a test the next day. _____

55. College professors like it when you seem interested in their class. _____

At a Glance

My name is _____. I am _____ years old.

I am or will be graduating high school in (month/year) _____.

I plan on attending college directly after high school.   ___yes   ___ no
If no, then my plan for after high school is to _____
_____
_____
_____

If yes, the name of the college(s) I am interested in is/are _____
_____

I have already requested and/or completed a college application? ___yes   ___ no

I will send my College Application in by (month/year) _____.

I have already taken the SAT/ACT.   ___yes   ___ no

If no, I will schedule to take it by (month/year) _____.

I want to start my first college semester in _____.

My major will be _____ in the school of _____.

The degree that I will pursue is a(n) (AA, AS, BA, BS) _____.

If I go to college for two or four years consecutively, I will graduate in (month and year) _____.

One a scale of 1-10, indicate how serious you are about going to college and earning your degree? _____.

Dr. Mia Y. Merritt, M&M Motivating
Life After High School: Valuable Life Skills for the Goal-Oriented Achiever!

Time to Reflect

It has been statistically proven that a college education can change the quality of a person's life drastically. In light of what you have learned about going to college, share how you feel your life can change just by earning your college degree.

_____

_____

_____

_____

_____

_____

_____

_____

_____

_____

_____

_____

_____

_____

_____

_____

_____

Check List
- ✓ Decided on a college or university
- ✓ Decided on a major
- ✓ Schedule to take the SAT/ACT
- ✓ Meet w/ Financial Aid Advisor at the university
- ✓ Gather admissions requirements
- ✓ Fill out my FAFSA
- ✓ Decide on how many classes to take per semester
- ✓ Register for classes on time
- ✓ Get all books needed for classes
- ✓ Schedule time to study and read
- ✓ Determine to graduate with my college degree!

Chapter 1 Answer Key

1. On the lines below, very briefly write where you will be and what you will be doing next year this time.

   Answers will vary

2. If you already know the college you want to attend, write the name and whether it is public or private and why you chose this particular school.

   Answers will vary

3. Name at least five benefits of going to college?

   Answers may vary, but may include:

   - ✓ **longer life spans**
   - ✓ **access to better health care**
   - ✓ **greater economic stability and security**
   - ✓ **better employment and greater job satisfaction**
   - ✓ **less dependency on government assistance**
   - ✓ **greater use of seat belts**
   - ✓ **more continuing education**
   - ✓ **more book purchases**
   - ✓ **higher voting rates**
   - ✓ **greater knowledge of politics and government**
   - ✓ **greater community service and leadership**
   - ✓ **increased self-confidence**
   - ✓ **less criminal activity and incarceration**
   - ✓ **Earn more money than you would without a college degree**
   - ✓ **Strengthen analytical and reasoning skills**
   - ✓ **Appreciate, understand and accept different points of view on a variety of different issues**
   - ✓ **Enhance your verbal expression and critical thinking skills**
   - ✓ **Increase your conversational and writing skills**
   - ✓ **Expand your understanding of the world and community from a global perspective**
   - ✓ **Broaden your social horizons**
   - ✓ **Opens the door for better job opportunities**
   - ✓ **Develop life-long friendships that you will cherish for a lifetime**

4. What are some of the health advantages that college students have over non-college degree holders?

   Answers may vary, but may include:
   - ✓ **longer life spans**
   - ✓ **access to better health care**
   - ✓ **more routine exams**
   - ✓

5. What is the difference between a public and a private college?
   - ✓ **Private colleges are more expensive than public colleges**

- ✓ Public colleges (also known as state colleges) are less expensive than private colleges
- ✓ The state gives funding and support to public colleges
- ✓ Private colleges rely on tuition and monetary gifts to sustain their operations

6. What are two advantages of attending a public university?
    - ✓ **Answers will vary, but may include:**
    - ✓ **lower tuition than private schools**
    - ✓ **stay close to home**

7. What are two disadvantages of attending a public university?
    - ✓ **You must remain within your home state in order to receive the highest tuition benefits reduces the choices of different colleges to choose from.**

8. What are two advantages of attending a private university?
    - ✓ **The power of "name recognition" among potential employers**
    - ✓ **Often draw high-quality faculty across the disciplines as well.**

9. What are two disadvantages of attending a private university?
    - ✓ **Private schools are often the most expensive**
    - ✓ **You must consider whether the debt you will incur will be offset by the money you will make in your potential career**

10-12 **Answers will vary**

13. Why should you not go into college with an "undeclared" major?

    Because time and money could be wasted while you are haphazardly taking unnecessary courses and ultimately wasting time.

14. Name three things that your college Academic Advisor does for you.
    - ✓ **He or she will meet with you to discuss your major**
    - ✓ **review the course selections with you**
    - ✓ **help you choose your classes**
    - ✓ **assist you in developing an academic plan**
    - ✓ **discuss your progress through a particular program**
    - ✓ **review your grades with you each semester**
    - ✓ **make sure that you are on path to graduating on time**
    - ✓ **talk to you about other concerns you may have**
    - ✓ **notify you if you are being placed on academic probation**
    - ✓ **explain the regulations and what must be done to return back to good academic standing.**

15-19 **Answers will vary**

20. What is academic probation?
    If you do not maintain a minimum Grade Point Average required by the university, you can be kicked out. Each university has a minimum GPA set forth

in their academic guidelines that all students must maintain or exceed. Typically, this G.P.A. is 3.0, which is a solid "B" and when students get close to falling below that, they are given an *Academic Warning*. When they fall below a 2.5, they are placed on *Academic Probation*.

21. What will you do to keep from getting on Academic Probation?

    Answers will vary, but may include any of the following:

    - ✓ Get to all your classes on time.
    - ✓ Get to know all your professors.
    - ✓ Take good notes.
    - ✓ Develop good study habits.
    - ✓ know your Course Guide & Syllabus.
    - ✓ Exceed all course expectations.
    - ✓ Don't wait until the last minute to get assignments done.
    - ✓ Stay organized.
    - ✓ Overcome your fears and master your weaknesses.
    - ✓ Do not overextend yourself.
    - ✓ Follow good rules of writing.
    - ✓ Practice good communication skills.
    - ✓ Always save your work and back it up.
    - ✓ Use your time wisely.

22. What is a Financial Aid Packet?
    A financial aid package is a combination of financial aid resources (grants, loans, work-study, etc.) that is put together by the Financial Aid Counselor at the college and is designed to meet your financial needs. The amount of awards and types of assistance in a package depends upon the total cost of attending that particular college, your individual needs, availability of funding, and outside funds available to you.

23. What is a FAFSA and the importance of it?
    To apply for financial aid from the federal government you must submit the Free Application for Federal Student Aid (FAFSA). There is no charge for submitting this form. The FAFSA is required by all states and many student assistance programs.

24. Name three advantages of living "**on**" campus.

    Answers will vary, but may include:
    - ✓ **Accessibility to the school**
    - ✓ **Full Experience of the College Life**
    - ✓ **Simplicity**

25. Name three advantages of living "**off**" campus.

    - ✓ **Privacy**
    - ✓ **Sense of Responsibility**
    - ✓ **Better study time**
    - ✓ **More space**
    - ✓ **More freedom**

26. Name at least five of the fastest growing and highest paying jobs from the Department of Labor's forecast through 2014.

Answers may vary, but may include:
- ✓ **Accountant**
- ✓ **Computer Software Engineer**
- ✓ **Dental Hygienist**
- ✓ **Health Diagnosis Technician**
- ✓ **Law Enforcement Officer**
- ✓ **Network Systems Administrator/Analyst**
- ✓ **Physical and Occupational Therapist**
- ✓ **Registered Nurse**
- ✓ **Teacher (all levels)**

27. Name at least five tips that you will apply while in college to make good grades.

Answers may vary, but may include:
- ✓ **Get to all your classes on time.**
- ✓ **Get to know all your professors.**
- ✓ **Take good notes.**
- ✓ **Develop good study habits.**
- ✓ **know your Course Guide & Syllabus.**
- ✓ **Exceed all course expectations.**
- ✓ **Don't wait until the last minute to get assignments done.**
- ✓ **Stay organized.**
- ✓ **Overcome your fears and master your weaknesses.**
- ✓ **Do not overextend yourself.**
- ✓ **Follow good rules of writing.**
- ✓ **Practice good communication skills.**
- ✓ **Always save your work and back it up.**
- ✓ **Use your time wisely.**

28. In your own words, what is the difference between the SAT and ACT?
Answers may vary, but may include:

AMERICAN COLLEGE TEST (ACT)	SCHOLASTIC APTITUDE TEST (SAT)
is knowledge-based	assesses natural abilities
contains English grammar skills	contains vocabulary skills
has math problems requiring students to show their work	is multiple choice only
has trigonometry problems	has basic geometry and Algebra 2
has a science reasoning component	does not have a science reasoning component

is more content-based	assesses critical thinking and problem solving skills
The highest score you can get is 36	The highest score you can get is 1600
is about three hours and 25 minutes	is about three hours and 45 minutes

29. What do BA and BS stand for?
    BA = Bachelor of Science
    BS = Bachelor of Arts

30. What do AA and AS stand for?
    AA: Associate of Arts
    AS: Associate of Science

31. What is the difference between the three degrees?
    A BA and BS are earned in four years. An AA or AS are earned in two years.

32. What is an internship?
    Internships give college students hands-on experience in their chosen major and allow them to explore and learn while gaining professional knowledge and exposure.

33. Name at least four benefits that internships can do for you.
    Answers may vary, but may include:
    - **Learn the intricacies of your chosen field**
    - **Apply classroom theory to real work situations**
    - **Discover your own skills and identify other talents in you**
    - **Learn about organizational cultures and diversity**
    - **Strengthen your written, oral and interpersonal skills**
    - **Find out if that selected career path is the one you really want to pursue**
    - **Experience the dynamics of working in a business environment**
    - **Enhance and strengthen your resume**
    - **Make contacts and references to gain future employment**
    - **Gain an increased awareness of skills, attributes, personal qualities and values**

34. Explain in your own words what a vocational/trade school is.
    Answers may vary, but may include:
    A vocational school, (also called a trade school or career school) is an institution where students are taught skills needed to perform a "specific" job in a "specific" field. These types of schools prepare students to find employment immediately after completing the courses. The jobs are usually based on manual or practical labor. The skills are usually non-academic, and are targeted to a specific trade, occupation, or vocation only. This type of education is referred to as "Technical Education" because

the person develops expertise in a particular group of techniques or technology directly.

35. What is the difference between a college and a vocational/trade school.
A college usually takes two or four years or longer. You can complete a vocational/trade school in less than two years. After completion at a college, you earn a college degree, but after completion at a trade school, you earn a certificate.

36. What are some of the questions you should ask why while seeking a good vocational/trade school?

Answers may vary, but may include:
- ✓ **How many students actually complete their programs?**
- ✓ **How many graduates are actually placed in their career field after completing a particular vocational/trade school?**
- ✓ **Are the facilities up-to-date?**
- ✓ **What extras does the school offer? Is there a career guidance office? If so, will they assist you in finding employment once you have completed your program? Will the school help you find internships while you are a student?**

37. Name two benefits of attending a vocational/trade school.

Answers may vary, but may include:
- ✓ **Higher hourly wages compared with those who only have a high school diploma**
- ✓ **Actively engaged in problem solving in the working environment**
- ✓ **Hands-on work responsibilities that allow application of knowledge**
- ✓ **Learn new work skills to meet requirements in an ever-changing work place**
- ✓ **Learn new skills for changing careers**
- ✓ **Typical 97% employment rate after graduation, with over 80% in the field of their certificate (U.S. Department of Education, 2006)**
- ✓ **Increased job skill transfer ability**
- ✓ **Increased job stability**
- ✓ **The ability to transfer to a four year college for a Bachelors Degree if desired**
- ✓ **The ability to earn a two year Associates Degree, if desired**

38. False	47. True
39. True	48. False
40. True	49. True
41. False	50. False
42. False	51. True
43. False	52. False
44. False	53. False
45. True	54. False
46. True	55. True

2
Career Preparation

Two Cents worth:

An honest days work doing something that you love makes for a sweet sleep.

Dr. Mia Y. Merritt

DATE _____

1. Write three things that you will do to prepare for a job interview.

   I. _____

   II. _____

   III. _____

2. Write three ways that you will find job openings.

   I. _____

   II. _____

   III. _____

3. After reading about the different resume formats, which format is the best one for you? Explain why on the next page

   ___Chronological:

   ___Functional:

   ___Combination:

_____

_____

4. Write three resume tips that you will use when developing your resume.

    I. _____

    II. _____

    III. _____

5. Why should a person not use educational dates longer than ten years old?

_____

_____

6. On the lines below, write the e-mail address(es) that you will give to potential employers to contact you. Is your e-mail address *name* appropriate to give to a potential employer?

_____

_____

7. Why is it important to be patient while waiting in the lobby to be called for your interview?

_____

_____

_____

8. While waiting to be called, what are some things that you can do that shows patience?

_____

_____

_____

9. Why do potential employers sometimes check your credit history as part of the application process?

_____

_____

_____

10. Will your background check come back clean? __ yes   __ no

11. If no, what is your plan "B" if questioned about any arrests? Check here if N/A ___

_____

_____

_____

12. If a potential employer was to check your Myspace, Facebook, Linkedin or Twitter postings, would you be embarrassed by what they would read?   __ yes   __ no

13. Why is it important to watch what you post and write on the internet?

_____

_____

_____

14. Do you know of any situations where a person's background came back to hurt them? If so describe it briefly below (the example can be a personal one or heard of).

_____

_____

_____

15. Why should you not lie on a job application?

_____

_____

16. What is your (realistic) ideal job to have?

_____

_____

17. What are your ideal work hours?

_____

18. What is a realistic starting salary that you would like to have?_____

19. What are you prepared to do to secure this kind of job?

_____

_____

20. How many hours a day are you prepared to invest in finding this ideal job?_____

MULTIPLE CHOICE

21. What are the best colors to wear on an interview?

    a. light colors   b. fluorescent colors   c. dark colors

22. The best kind of shoes to wear on an interview are:

    a. open-toe   b. boots   c. closed-in

23. When is it a good idea to shake the interviewer's hand?

    a. before the interview   b. after the interview   c. before or after

24. What would be the best form of eye contact?

    a. look down   b. look only at the person talking to you

    c. look around at everyone in the room while speaking

25. Would it be appropriate to send a "Thank you" card after your interview?

    ___ **Yes**   ___ **no**

ANSWER THE FOLLOWING QUESTIONS THE WAY YOU WOULD IN AN INTERVIEW:

26. Tell us a little about yourself.

_____

_____

_____

_____

27. What are your strengths?

_____

_____

_____

28. What are your weaknesses?

_____

_____

_____

29. Name at least four questions that employers are prohibited from asking you.

    I. _____

   II. _____

  III. _____

  IV. _____

30. What is the name of the act that protects individuals over 40 years old from being discriminated against?

_____

Dr. Mia Y. Merritt, M&M Motivating
Life After High School: Valuable Life Skills for the Goal-Oriented Achiever!

Time to Reflect

Working is a mandatory part of life. There is no way that you become an adult and never have to work to earn a living. Even if you were born into wealth and power, you still must work to sustain the family's wealth. Since you will be working much longer than you are retired, then you should definitely have a job that you love. On the lines below, share why having a fulfilling career is important to you and what you will do to climb the ladder of upward mobility while on this job that you love.

FUNCTIONAL RESUME EXAMPLE

Maria Hernandez
1525 Jackson Street, City, NY 11111
Phone: 555-555-5555
Email: jadelo@bac.net

OBJECTIVE
To obtain a position where I can maximize my multilayer of management skills, quality assurance, program development, training experience, customer service and a successful track record in the Blood Banking care environment.

SUMMARY OF QUALIFICATIONS
Results-oriented, high-energy, hands-on professional, with a successful record of accomplishments in the blood banking, training and communication transmission industries. Experience in phlebotomy, blood banking industry, training, quality assurance and customer service with focus on providing the recipient with the highest quality blood product, fully compliant with FDA cGMP, Code of Federal Regulations, AABB accreditation and California state laws.

Major strengths include strong leadership, excellent communication skills, competent, strong team player, attention to detail, dutiful respect for compliance in all regulated environment and supervisory skills including hiring, termination, scheduling, training, payroll and other administrative tasks. Thorough knowledge of current manufacturing practices and a clear vision to accomplish the company goals. Computer and Internet literate

PROFESSIONAL ACCOMPLISHMENTS

Program/Project Manager
Facilitated educational projects successfully over the past two years for Northern California blood centers, a FDA regulated manufacturing environment, as pertaining to cGMP, CFR's, CA state and American Association of Blood Bank (AABB) regulations and assure compliance with 22 organization quality systems.

Provided daily operational review/quality control of education accountability as it relates to imposed government regulatory requirements in a medical environment.
Assisted other team members in veni-punctures, donor reaction care and providing licensed staffing an extension in their duties by managing the blood services regulations documentation (BSD's) while assigned to the self-contained blood mobile unit (SCU).
Successfully supervised contract support for six AT&T Broadband systems located in the Bay Area. Provided customer intervention/resolution, training in telephony and customer care, Manpower Scheduling, Quality Control, Payroll and special projects/plant extensions and evaluations to ensure proper end-of-line and demarkcation signal.

Reduced employee turnovers, introduced two-way communication to field employees, enhanced employee appearance and spearheaded the implementation of employee (health) benefits.

Chief point of contact for the AT&T telephone and the ABC Affiliated TV stations as it relates to complaints and diagnosing communicational problems either at the site or remote broadcasting. Also tested/repaired prototype equipment for possible consideration or for future use. Reviewed FAA safety requirements and procedures to ensure compliance for aircraft and passenger safety.
Communication expert and programming specialist for the intermediate range Lance and Persian missile systems. Trained to operate and repair the (FDC) fire direction control computer system and field satellite communications.
Supervised and maintained the position of System Technician in charge of status monitoring and the integration of monitoring devices in nodes and power supplies. For the reception and transmission of telemetry to the network operation centers (NOC's) located in Denver, CO and Fremont, CA. Designed plant extensions, improved the paper flow and inventory control for the warehouse. Provided preventative maintenance at the system level, face to face customer interaction when required and traveled to several telephony/@home systems in the U.S. for evaluation and suggestions in using the status monitoring equipment.

Education
Associate of Arts, Administration of Justice
San Jose University, San Jose, CA

CHRONOLOGICAL RESUME EXAMPLE

Michael H. Jones
156 Everglades Lane
Boston, MA 45963
986-512-4536 (home)   566.486.2222 (cell)
Mhjones@vacapp.com

EXPERIENCE

Key Holder, Montblanc
April 2001 - February 2005

- Opened new specialty boutique
- Placed orders to restock merchandise and handled receiving of products
- Managed payroll, scheduling, reports, email, inventory, and maintained clientele book and records
- Integrated new register functions
- Extensive work with visual standards and merchandising high-ticket items

Sales Associate, Nordstrom - Collectors and Couture Departments
July 1999 - April 2001

- Merchandised designer women's wear
- Set-up trunk shows and attended clinics for new incoming fashion lines
- Worked with tailors and seamstresses for fittings
- Scheduled private shopping appointments with high-end customers

Bartender
Jigg's Corner
February 1997 - July 1999

- Provide customer service in fast-paced bar atmosphere
- Maintain and restock inventory
- Administrative responsibilities include processing hour and tip information for payroll and closing register

EDUCATION

Ramapo College, Arlington, Virginia

Computer Skills

- Proficient with Microsoft Word, Excel, and PowerPoint, and Internet

COMBINATION RESUME EXAMPLE

Phillip Boston
789 W. 24th Parkway
Jacksonville, FL 33716-2502
(727) 578-0191
Pboston@tampabay.rr.com

I am interested in pursuing a career in software development. I consider myself a fast learner and a team player. I feel that I can make a contribution to any Implementation Services department.

Computer Experience

Machines: IBM PC compatibles, Rockwell ACD, Macintosh
Languages: VBA, BASIC, Turbo Pascal, DB/c, Turbo C, COBOL
Programs: MS Access, MS Word, MS Excel, MS Outlook, Crystal Reports, MS Internet Explorer, Netscape
Operating Systems: MS Vista, MS XP, MS Windows1, SCO UNIX, MS DOS
Hardware: Experienced with installation of mother boards, SIMM chips, internal/external modems, NICs, SCSI and IDE hard disks, SCSI floppy drives, SCSI I/O ports, and various printer configurations.

Experience

1998 to Present Med Resorts International, Clearwater, FL
Systems Developer

Responsible for migration of extensive filePro database to MS Access utilizing tables, queries, forms, reports, macros, modules, and VBA. Troubleshoot and maintain existing MS Access database for Telemarketing Dept. Troubleshoot and diagnose UNIX, filePro, PC, and MS Windows related problems for in-house staff.

1995 to 1998 Lasergate Systems, Clearwater, FL

Support Engineer

Troubleshoot and debug minor program bugs. Modify existing programs with enhancements. Implement fixes and enhancements. Design, create, and implement ticket designs. Perform remote upgrades of ProtoBase and Select-a-Seat. Resolve problems and questions from Technical Support. Provide documentation. Assist Select-a-Seat Team Leader with creation and testing of new software.

Previous positions:
Senior Technical Support Representative
Technical Support Representative
Technical Support Operator
1988 to 1995 Home Shopping Network, St. Petersburg, FL

Help Desk Supervisor

Manage the Help Desk function as well as prioritizing, resolving, recognizing, and routing end-user computer problems. Establish and document policy and procedure.

Previous positions:
Help Desk Operator II
Assistant Data Systems Analyst
Telecommunications Systems Operator
Customer Service Phone Monitor Trainer
Customer Service Representative
Network Representative

Education
St. Petersburg Jr. College, St. Petersburg, FL
1986 to 1994
Major: A.S. Computer Programming and Analysis
GPA: 3.70
Warner Robins High School, Warner Robins, GA
1972 to 1975
Recipient of Who's Who in American High Schools

References

Cover Letter Example

Chastidy TreeRound
15963 NW. 18 Ct, Miami, FL 33301
(786) 954-4127 cell or (305) 624-6808 home
chastidytreer@yahoo.com

December 7, 2010

Ms. Andrea Watson
Miami-Dade Federal Credit Union
Human Resource Director
1500 NW 107th Ave
Miami, FL 33172

Dear Ms. Watson,

As a result of seeing your advertisement for the Bank Teller position on Craig's List, I have attached my resume, which outlines my experiences and qualifications for the position advertised.
I currently manage cash amounts ranging from $2,500-$3,000 on a daily basis as a cashier at Publix Grocery Store. I've worked in this capacity for almost three years, and I have proven my competence, reliability, and loyalty in this position. My desire for upward mobility in my area of proficiency has led me to apply for the Bank Teller Position at your prestigious institution. I've effectively solved challenges that have presented themselves to me and my skill of being proactive has allowed me to tackle potential problems from occurring.

I look forward to meeting with you in an interview setting to explore the career opportunities that may be available to me as a Bank Teller at your fine institution. I can be contacted at the above address and phone number to schedule an interview.
I look forward to meeting you and I thank you in advance for considering my credentials for the position posted.

Respectfully,

Chastidy Treeround

Check List
- ✓ Develop an appropriate eye-catching resume.
- ✓ Have at least two people proof-read my resume for mistakes and/or suggestions.
- ✓ Search the web or other sources for job openings in my field.
- ✓ Submit my resume and cover letter in the manner suggested by the company.
- ✓ Practice answering common questions that may be asked about my strengths, weaknesses and abilities.
- ✓ Practice answering interview questions either in a mirror or with family or friends.
- ✓ Stay encouraged and be confident that I will secure the right job for me!

Chapter 2 Answer Key

1. Write three things that you are going to do to prepare for getting an interview.
   Answers may vary, but may include any of the following:
   - **Practice interviewing skills**
   - **Research the company on the internet**
   - **Prepare the right clothes to wear**
   - **Make sure my resume and other documents are ready to present**
   - **Bring a good book in case you have to wait**
   - **Know what my strengths and weaknesses are**

2. Write three ways that you can find job openings.
   Answers may vary, but may include any of the following:
   - **Search Career websites on the internet**
   - **Check the career center at the school**
   - **Search the local newspapers**
   - **Visit certain businesses**
   - **Trade magazines**

3. After reading about the different resume formats, which format is the best way for you to write your resume? Explain why.
   Answers may vary, but must include one of the following:
   - **Chronological**
   - **Functional**
   - **Combination**

4. Write three resume tips that you will use when developing your resume.
   Answers may vary, but may include any of the following:
   - **Do not include dates older than 10 years old**
   - **Be consistent throughout the resume**
   - **Do not use 1st, 2nd or 3rd person references**
   - **Include first and last name in the electronic file**
   - **Do a spell check**
   - **Prepare your cover letter**

5. Why should a person not use educational dates longer than ten years old?
   Because it gives an indication of one's age.

6. On the lines below, write the e-mail address(es) that you will give to potential employers to contact you. Is your e-mail address name appropriate to give to a potential employer?
   Answers will vary

7. Why is it important to be patient while waiting in the lobby to be called for your interview?
   Answers may vary, but may include any of the following:
   - **Because include dates older than 10 years old**
   - **Be consistent throughout the resume**

8. While waiting to be called, what are some things that you can do that shows patience?
   Answers may vary, but may include any of the following:
   - ✓ **Read a book**
   - ✓ **Sit patiently with your hands folded**
   - ✓ **Play a game on your cell phone**
   - ✓ **Write in your journal**

9. Why do potential employers sometimes check your credit history as part of the application process?
   Because they want to make sure that the amount of money the position offers will be sufficient to pay your bills.

10. Will your background check come back clean? __ yes   __ no
    Answers will vary

11. If no, what is your plan "B" if questioned about any arrests? Check here if N/A ___
    Answers will vary

12. If a potential employer was to check your Myspace, Facebook, or Twitter postings, would you be embarrassed by what they would find? __ yes __ no
    Answers will vary

13. Why is it important to watch what you post and write on the internet?
    Because what you write or say can come back to haunt you and prevent you from getting a decent job or political office.

14. Do you know of any situations where a person's background came back to haunt them? If so describe it briefly below (can be personal or heard of).
    Answers will vary

15. Why should you not lie on a job application?
    Because when the records come back, and you have lied, it makes you look dishonest and may prevent you from securing the job.

16. What is your (realistic) ideal job to have?
    Answers will vary

17. What are your ideal work hours?
    Answers will vary

18. What is a realistic starting salary that you would like to have?
    Answers will vary

19. What are you prepared to do to secure this kind of job?
    Answers will vary

20. How many hours a day are you prepared to invest in finding this ideal job?
Answers will vary

21. What are the best colors to wear on an interview?
c. Dark colors

22. The best kind of shoes to wear on an interview are:
c. Closed in

23. When is it a good idea to shake the interviewer's hand?
c. before or after

24. What would be the best form of eye contact?
c. look around at everyone in the room while speaking

25. Would it be appropriate to send a "Thank you" card after the interview?
Yes it is appropriate

26. Tell us a little about yourself.
Answers will vary

27. What are your strengths?
Answers will vary

28. What are your weaknesses?
Answers will vary

29. Name at least four questions that employers are prohibited from asking you.
Answers may include four of the following:

- ✓ How old are you?
- ✓ Are you married?
- ✓ Are you a U.S. citizen?
- ✓ Do you have any disabilities?
- ✓ Do you take drugs, smoke or drink?
- ✓ What religion do you practice?
- ✓ What is your race?
- ✓ Are you pregnant?

30. What is the name of the act that protects individuals 40 years or older from being discriminated against?

The *Age Discrimination Employment Act of 1967* (ADEA)

3
Dating & Relationships

Two Cents worth:

A true friend is someone who thinks that you are a good egg even though he knows that you are slightly cracked.

Bernard Meltzer

DATE _____

1. What does casual dating mean?

   _____

   _____

   _____

2. What first attracts you to a person as a potential mate?

   _____

   _____

   _____

3. Is a person's conversation important to you? Why or why not?

   ___Yes   ___ No

   _____

   _____

   _____

4. What are the most important attributes of friendship to you?

_____

_____

_____

5. Does a person need to be on the same mental and educational level as you in order for you to date them? Why or why not?

                    ___ **Yes**   ___ **No**

_____

_____

_____

6. What are five important attributes that a person should possess in order for you to date them?

    I. _____

    II. _____

    III. _____

    IV. _____

    V. _____

7. List three main elements that a relationship should have in order to be healthy.

    I. _____

    II. _____

    III. _____

8. What good qualities do you think you bring to a relationship?

    I. _____

      II. _____

      III. _____

      IV. _____

9. What are some faults you need to work on so they won't become a problem in a relationship?

_____

_____

_____

10. On a scale of 1-5 (five being the most important), how important is intimacy and romance to you in a relationship?   1 __ 2 __ 3 __ 4 __ 5 __

11. When things bother you, do you like talking them out or do you avoid facing the concerns? Why or why not?

_____

_____

_____

12. Do you think your answer above is the best way to deal with your concerns? Why or why not?

_____

_____

_____

13. Have you ever been in love? How do you know?

                ___Yes   ___No

_____

_____

_____

14. Do you still have feelings for the person you were in love with? How do you know? Explain why you are not still together.

                            ___Yes   ___ No

_____

_____

_____

15. Do you think you love easily or is it difficult to earn your love? Explain your answer.

_____

_____

_____

16. Have you ever had a broken heart? ___Yes   ___ No. If yes, how did it feel?

_____

_____

_____

17. Are you COMPLETELY over your broken heart? Explain how you know.

_____

_____

_____

18. Have you ever been in an abuse relationship? If yes, what kind of abuse was it? (Physical Abuse, Sexual Abuse, Psychological/Emotional/Mental Abuse, Financial Abuse, Neglect, Religious Abuse).

_____

_____

_____

19. Do you think you contributed to the abuse in any way? If yes, please explain.

_____

_____

_____

20. Are you willing to accept the fact that you were not responsible for someone else's choice to be abusive towards you? __Yes ___ No.   Explain your answer.

_____

_____

_____

21. How did being abused make you feel? _____

_____

_____

_____

22. How does it make you feel now as you reflect back on it?

_____

_____

_____

23. Do you think the abuse has made you a different person? Please explain.

_____

_____

_____

24. If the abuse you endured has impacted you negatively, then explain what you are going to do from this point forward to begin walking in self-confidence, self-assurance and self-belief in the greatness and power that resides within you?

25. How will you help someone leave an abusive situation?

26. Do you think that you carry some emotional baggage from the abusive relationship of your past? ___Yes ___ No   Please explain your answer on the lines below.

27. Is there some other traumatic experience that you endured in your past that you are shameful of, guilty of, grief-stricken by or victimized by? If you choose, you may write it down on the lines below. If you are not ready to release it by writing it down, you may wait until you are ready and go to the next question (writing is a form of therapy and you will feel a sense of relief after getting it out of you this way).

28. Write how you felt as you experienced this situation.

29. How do you feel about that situation now?

30. Do you think you are healed? If not, how will you seek healing? If yes, how do you know that you are healed?

31. Describe a past relationship that ended on a sour note. (It could be a friendship or a relationship).

    Person's Name: _____ Nature of Relationship: friend, mate, other

    Why did the relationship end?

32. Do you think emotional baggage played a role in any way (either yours or theirs)?

_____

_____

_____

33. In looking back, how could it have ended differently?

_____

_____

_____

34. Are you cordial with the person now? __Yes ___ No.

35. If no, would you be willing to contact them and reconcile? __Yes ___ No.
Explain your answer:

_____

_____

_____

TRUE/FALSE

36. It is healthy to hold in bad experiences from the past. _____

37. It is not possible to achieve your goals without the help of others. _____

38. People with the same goals, intentions, and similar personalities usually attract each other. _____

39. Getting rejected does not mean that anything is wrong with you. It just means that the person who rejected you was not the one for you. _____

40. An abusive relationship is a dysfunctional relationship. _____

Time to Reflect

After reading the chapter on relationships, you learned what a healthy relationship looks like and what a dysfunctional one looks like. On the lines below, share your thoughts on the kind relationships you would like to have in your life and what you are willing to do to maintain those relationships.

_____

_____

_____

_____

_____

_____

_____

_____

_____

_____

_____

_____

_____

_____

_____

_____

Self-check
- ✓ Take a look inward and identify my flaws
- ✓ Work on eliminating my flaws and work on new qualities
- ✓ Take responsibility for the mistakes I've made in the past
- ✓ Forgive myself for the mistakes I've made in my life
- ✓ Face any abuse that I've endured in the past
- ✓ Talk through that abuse with someone trustworthy
- ✓ Work on forgiving the person who abused me
- ✓ Walk in the confidence that I am worthy of true happiness, prosperity and love
- ✓ Begin working on achieving new goals
- ✓ Become a new person!

Chapter 3 Answer Key

1. What does casual sex mean?

Casual sex refers to sexual encounters with strangers, friends, acquaintances, or people who agree to have sex with no emotional ties or commitment. It is done in the context of an agreement where the sex is only an activity that mainly satisfies a sexual desire or physical attraction. Unfortunately, casual sex is something that has become very common among teens and young adults.

2. What first attracts you to a person?

Answers will vary for questions 2-35.

36. It is healthy to hold in bad experiences from the past.

FALSE

37. It is not possible to achieve your goals without the help of others.

TRUE

38. People with the same goals, intentions, and similar personalities usually attract each other.
TRUE

39. Getting rejected does not mean that anything is wrong with you. It just
TRUE

40. An abuse relationship is a dysfunctional relationship.

TRUE

Dr. Mia Y. Merritt, M&M Motivating
Life After High School: Valuable Life Skills for the Goal-Oriented Achiever!

4
Setting Goals & Strategic Planning

Two Cents worth:

The secret to productive goal setting is establishing clearly defined goals, writing Them down and then focusing on them several times a day with words and emotions as if you've already achieved them.

Anonymous

Setting goals gives meaning to your life. With goals to work towards, you are always striving to grow, develop, and get better.

DATE _____

What you see with the natural eye already exists in the physical world, but what you see when you visualize, already exists in the spiritual world. You must bring what you see in the mental world out of the invisible into the visible.

Charles Haanal

Plan for Prosperity and Abundance

People are looking at you and wondering if you truly believe in your vision, your goals, and your dreams. If you are not positive, if you are not confident, if you are not excited about your own goals, how can you expect anyone else to be excited for you? When you work with diligence towards your goals, people notice, and they support you and your vision. Everything you do will make an impression on others. Therefore, it is of the utmost importance that you begin to value yourself as an individual worthy of accomplishing great things.

Part A:

On the lines below, identify at least three major goals in each area that you would like to accomplish within the next six months. Make sure that your goals are challenging and realistic.

Under each goal, there are spaces provided for you to write action plans to describe how you will accomplish these goals. For instance, if your goal was to take two classes at the local university, then your goal and action plan should look something like this:

EDUCATIONAL GOAL:
1. Complete two classes at the local university.

Action Plan:
    a. Register for classes during the Fall registration
    b. Purchase books needed for both classes.

ON THE LINES BELOW, DEVELOP YOUR MEANINGFUL, ACHIEVABLE GOALS IN EACH CATEGORY TO ACHIEVE IN THE NEXT SIX MONTHS:

SPIRITUAL GOALS:

1. _____

    Action Plan _____

2. _____

    Action Plan _____

3. _____

    Action Plan _____

EDUCATIONAL GOALS:

1. _____

    Action Plan _____

2. _____

    Action Plan _____

3. _____

    Action Plan _____

FUTURE CAREER GOALS:

1. _____

   Action Plan _____

2. _____

   Action Plan _____

3. _____

   Action Plan _____

FINANCIAL GOALS:

1. _____

   Action Plan _____

2. _____

   Action Plan _____

3. _____

   Action Plan _____

HEALTH GOALS:

1. _____

   Action Plan _____

2. _____

   Action Plan _____

3. _____

   Action Plan _____

PERSONAL GOALS:

1. _____

Action Plan _____

2. _____

    Action Plan _____

3. _____

    Action Plan _____

Be sure to review your goals on a weekly basis to make sure you are on tract to achieving them.

> *When you have a clear vision of the person you intend to become and you have distinct goals written to help you become that person, your life has meaning. Small, insignificant things no longer bother you because your eyes are on the goals in front of you.*

You may use the format below for writing one year goals, monthly goals or weekly goals. They may look something like this:

Yearly Goals	**Monthly Goals**	**Weekly Goals**

Spiritual:
1.
2.
Financial:
1.
2.
Educational:
1.
2.
    Etc.
	Spiritual:
	1.
	2.
	Financial:
	1.
	2.
	Educational:
	1.
	2.
	    Etc.
		Spiritual:
		1.
		2.
		Financial:
		1.
		2.
		Educational:
		1.
		2.
		    Etc.

Your motivation is increased when you write a personal mission statement for your life. Writing an affirmation takes time. It requires you to look deep inside yourself and identify your strengths and weaknesses. Going deep inside and identifying the less attractive stuff can be a humbling, yet beneficial and worthwhile undertaking. It requires soul-searching. Write down your strengths and weaknesses. Go deep within yourself and write down what you find out. Then, identify what you want out of life and what role you want to play in the lives of those with whom you love and interact. Your goals must be clearly defined, realistic, meaningful, and acted upon.

Make the Application:
Write your own personal affirmation.
Use as many sheets of paper as needed to write it.
This is the ideal person that you want to become.

PERSONAL LIFE AFFIRMATION FOR:

_____

After you have written your affirmation, make several copies of it. Post one up in your bathroom so that you can see it in the mornings. Take one with you to work or school so that you may read it at your leisure. Keep one in your notebook, so that as you think about it, you can ponder upon it. Continue to repeat this affirmation everyday until it becomes a habit so strong that your subconsciousness picks it up. You will soon see how you start becoming this person that you are visualizing. You will begin to attract people, circumstances, things, and events to you resulting from the powerful words that you are putting out into to universe.

Part B: POSITIVE THINKING

What things can you put into place to train your mind to think positive about yourself and the world around you? What are some things you can do to bring laughter and joy into your life?

1. On the lines below, write three short affirmations that you can say on a daily basis to keep your mind positive (other than your personal affirmation).

    I. _____

    II. _____

    III. _____

2. What are other things that you can do to focus on positive things?

    I. _____

    II. _____

    III. _____

3. What are the things that bring you joy, laughter, and make you smile?

    I. _____

    II. _____

    III. _____

4. How often do you do the things that bring you joy?

_____

_____

Time to Reflect

It has been said that only 3% of Americans actually sit down and plan out their life by writing goals. They then go a step further and write action plans for accomplishing those goals. Write on the lines below how you think setting goals will help you to personally develop your life and lead you to the path of prosperity.

Chapter 4 Answer Key

All answers from chapter four are based on individual responses and will vary.

Self-check
- ✓ Develop meaningful short term and long term goals that will add value to my life
- ✓ Create an action plan for carrying out each of my goals
- ✓ Establish timelines and target dates for the completion of my goals
- ✓ Write my personal mission statement (affirmation) of the kind of person that I want to become
- ✓ Post my affirmation in visible places where I can see it
- ✓ Recite my personal affirmation at least once daily
- ✓ Keep my mind on positive things and eliminate negative thoughts when they enter my mind

5
Cultivating Your Gifts

Two Cents worth:

Everything that lives has periods of birth, growth, fruitage, and decline. The periods of growth and fruitage should far outweigh every other area in your life. You must unfold all the gifts inside of you.

Charles Haanel

DATE _____

1. What gift, talent, or skill do you have that you are not allowing to express in your life?

    i. _____

    ii. _____

    iii. _____

2. What are your greatest skills?

    i. _____

    ii. _____

    iii. _____

3. Why have you not allowed this talent or skill to express through you on a frequent and consistent basis?

    i. _____

    ii. _____

    iii. _____

4. What can you begin to do *today* to start cultivating your gifts, talents, and skills?

_____

_____

_____

5. In what ways can you benefit by expressing your gifts, talents, and skills?

_____

_____

_____

6. What do you think will happen to your gifts, talents, and skills if you don't use them?

_____

_____

_____

7. Do you have a fear of expressing your gifts, talents, and skills? ___ yes ___ no. Explain

_____

_____

_____

8. On the lines below, describe yourself in three adjectives. Don't think too hard about it. Just write the first three words that come to your mind. These are usually the most honest.

    i. _____

    ii. _____

    iii. _____

9. If someone were to ask you to tell them a little about yourself, what would you say? Write how you would describe yourself on the lines that follow:

_____

_____

> *In writing your three adjectives and describing yourself, did you depict yourself in terms of your appearance, your abilities, your outlook on life, or a combination of those things? Most people would assess themselves in terms of the roles they play in the lives of others, (i.e. a daughter, a son, a parent, a spouse, an employee, or a friend). Some of your word choices probably included your relationships with others (i.e. loyal, faithful, caring, etc.) This simple exercise helps you to define the person you "think" you are.*

10. Name three unique characteristics about yourself that set you apart from others?

   i. _____

   ii. _____

   iii. _____

11. Write down three of your strengths.

   i. _____

   ii. _____

   iii. _____

12. Why do you feel that these are strengths?

_____

_____

_____

13. On the lines below, write down three of your weaknesses.

   i. _____

   ii. _____

iii. _____

14. Why do you feel that these are weaknesses?

_____

_____

_____

15. What are your greatest fears?

_____

_____

_____

16. From where or how do you think these fears came?

_____

_____

_____

17. How do you think you can overcome your fears?

_____

_____

_____

18. How will you overcome them?

_____

_____

_____

F E A R: **F**alse **E**xpectations **A**ppearing **R**eal.

Once you overcome your "false expectations" and pursue your goals with running shoes on, you will begin to do things you never imagined were possible. Fearlessness removes all fear!

One of the most profound quotes on fear that I have ever read comes from **Marianne Williamson** in the following.

OUR DEEPEST FEAR

Our deepest fear is not that we are inadequate. Our deepest fear is that we are powerful beyond measure.
It is our light, not our darkness that most frightens us. We ask ourselves, Who am I to be brilliant, gorgeous, talented, and fabulous?
Actually, who are you not to be?
You are a child of God.
Your playing small does not serve the world. There is nothing enlightened about shrinking so that other people won't feel insecure around you. We are all meant to shine, as children do.
We were born to make manifest the glory of God that is within us.
It's not just in some of us; it's in everyone. And as we let our own light shine, we unconsciously give other people permission to do the same.
As we are liberated from our own fear, our presence automatically liberates others.

Marianne Williamson

Part B:

Dave Weber, author of the book *Sticks and Stones* defined seven concepts of self. He states that each of these concepts lives inside of us and help define the person we are. According to him, our composite as human beings results from the integration of the seven concepts. Those concepts are the following:

The Seven Me's

- The Me I Think I am
- The Me I Really am
- The Me I Use to Be
- The Me That Others see
- The Me I Try to Project
- The Me Others Try to Make Me
- The Me I Want to Be

You probably never really looked at your life this way, but if you are honest with yourself, you can agree that there are at least five of these "Me's" in you. On the lines below, try and describe each one.

1. The "Me" I Think I am.

_____
_____
_____
_____

2. The "Me" I really am.

_____
_____
_____
_____

3. The "Me" I Use to be.

_____
_____
_____

4. The "Me" that others see.

_____
_____
_____
_____

5. The "Me I try to project.

_____
_____
_____
_____

6. The "Me" that others try to make me.

_____
_____
_____
_____

7. The "Me I want to be.

_____
_____
_____
_____

Part C:
This next exercise is not for you. It is for you to take to someone who knows you well. Remember that the way you see yourself is not always how others see you. In fact, it can be drastically different. Therefore, follow the directions below in order to give you a clearer picture of how others see you.

Directions: Give the next three pages to three people who know you. They will answer the questions based on how they see you. Do not get upset by their honest answers. Honestly sometimes brings enlightenment and change. ☺

Name of Evaluator: _____ **Date:** _____

Relationship to me: _____ **How long have you known me?** _____

Use three adjectives to describe me.

1. _____

2. _____

3. _____

What would you say are my best qualities? _____
_____
_____

What do you see as my strengths? _____
_____
_____

What do you see as a fault (or faults) that I can work on?
_____
_____

How would you describe my moods?

__ stable   __ pleasant   __ sometimes pleasant   __ always pleasant   __ moody

On the lines below, write your own personal message to me. _____
_____
_____
_____

Name of Evaluator: _____ **Date:** _____

Relationship to me: _____ **How long have you known me?** _____

Use three adjectives to describe me.

    1. _____

    2. _____

    3. _____

What would you say are my best qualities? _____

_____

_____

What do you see as my strengths? _____

_____

_____

What do you see as a fault (or faults) that I can work on?

_____

_____

How would you describe my moods?

__stable   __pleasant   ___ sometimes pleasant   ___ always pleasant   ___ moody

On the lines below, write your own personal message to me. _____

_____

_____

_____

Name of Evaluator: _____ **Date:** _____

Relationship to me: _____ **How long have you known me?** _____

Use three adjectives to describe me.

    4. _____

    5. _____

    6. _____

What would you say are my best qualities? _____

_____

_____

What do you see as my strengths? _____

_____

_____

What do you see as a fault (or faults) that I can work on?

_____

_____

How would you describe my moods?

__ stable __ pleasant __ sometimes pleasant __ always pleasant __ moody

On the lines below, write your own personal message to me. _____

_____

_____

_____

Time to Reflect

Describe your response to the entries that people wrote about you. How did reading their responses make you feel? Did you know they viewed you this way? Describe how you felt as you read the answers about you. Will it change you in any way?

Dr. Mia Y. Merritt, M&M Motivating
Life After High School: Valuable Life Skills for the Goal-Oriented Achiever!

Chapter 5 Answer Key

All answers for this chapter will vary.

Self-check
- ✓ I will identify all the things I do well and identify which are my skills and which are gifts.
- ✓ I will begin to cultivate my gifts by using them often.
- ✓ I will seek ways to make money by expressing my skills and gifts
- ✓ I will work on any fear that would stop me from expressing my skills and gifts.
- ✓ I will remind myself of my good qualities and express those qualities often.
- ✓ I will work on my weaknesses until they become strengths.
- ✓ I will remind myself that I am powerful beyond measure.
- ✓ I will analyze the answers that others wrote of me and seek to improve any weak areas.
- ✓ I will become a new person!

6
Your Credit Report

Two Cents worth:

The United States financial foundation is built upon credit, which faith that what is borrowed will be repaid with interest.

Dr. Mia Y. Merritt

DATE _____

1. In your own words, describe what financing means.

   _____
   _____
   _____

2. In your own words, describe what a Credit Report is.

   _____
   _____
   _____

3. What are the names of the three major credit bureaus in the United States?

   _____   _____   _____

4. What is the main function of Credit Bureaus?

   _____

_____

_____

5. What are the consequences of having a low Credit Rating (FICO score)?

_____

_____

_____

6. What is the name of the act that states that the information on your Credit Report must be complete and accurate?

_____

7. What can you do to dispute wrong information on your credit report?

_____

_____

_____

8. How is a FICO score calculated?

_____

_____

_____

9. Name the five areas that make up a credit score.

    I. _____

    II. _____

    III. _____

    IV. _____

V. _____

10. Explain what an Interest Rate is.

_____

_____

_____

Choose the best answer for each sentence.

11. An excellent FICO credit score is:

   a. 720-850   b. 500-619   c. 620-674

12. An "R1" rating on your report means.

   a. you make late payments   b. you pay over 30 days
         c. you make payments on time.

13. Your "Payment History" makes up what percentage of your credit report?

   a. 15%   b. 30%   c. 35%

14. The length of your credit history makes up what percentage of your credit report?

   a. 15%   b. 30%   c. 35%

15. The total amount owed makes up what percentage of your credit report?

   a. 15%   b. 30%   c. 35%

16. Name at least five things you can do to keep your credit in good standing.

   I. _____
   II. _____
   III. _____
   IV. _____
   V. _____

17. Name at least five things that can make your Credit Record bad.

   I. _____

   II. _____

   I. _____

   II. _____

   III. _____

18. In your opinion, what was the purpose of the Credit Card Accountability Responsibility and Disclosure Act?

_____

_____

_____

19. Name at least three components of the Credit Card Accountability Responsibility and Disclosure Act?

   i. _____

   ii. _____

   iii. _____

20. On the lines below, write at least three things that you are going to start doing immediately to increase your credit score.

   i. _____

   ii. _____

   iii. _____

If you are over 21 years of age, complete the exercises on the following page.

Request a copy of your Credit Report from each bureau and answer the following questions with your reports in hand.

I. The copy of the report I am looking at comes from _____

Based on this report, my FICO score is _____

This falls in the: EXCELLENT, GOOD, FAIR, POOR Range. (circle one)

I found the following discrepancies on this Credit Report.

1. _____

2. _____

3. _____

I will file a dispute within the next 30 days. ___ yes ___ no

II. The copy of the report that I am looking at comes from _____

Based on this report, my FICO score is _____

This falls in the: EXCELLENT, GOOD, FAIR, POOR Range. (circle one)

I found the following discrepancies on this Credit Report.

1. _____

2. _____

3. _____

I will file a dispute within the next 30 days. ___ yes ___ no

III. The copy of the report that I am looking at comes from _____

Based on this report, my FICO score is _____

This falls in the: EXCELLENT, GOOD, FAIR, POOR Range. (circle one)

I found the following discrepancies on this Credit Report.

1. _____

2. _____

3. _____

I will file a dispute within the next 30 days. ___ yes ___ no

Time to Reflect

Now that you have been given some essential information about the importance of your Credit Report, what are you prepared to do to ensure that your credit will become impeccable? Maintaining good credit will require self-discipline and careful spending habits. Are you prepared to do those things?

Self-check
- ✓ I will request my Credit Report at least once a year.
- ✓ I will put in the time and effort to correct all errors on my Credit Report.
- ✓ I will pay all my bills on time.
- ✓ I will seek to increase my FICO score by paying all outstanding debt.
- ✓ I will seek to pay all my credit cards down to less than 50% of the balance.
- ✓ I will seek to always keep a high Credit FICO score!

Chapter 6 Answer Key

1. In your own words, describe what financing means.
Financing basically means to borrow money from a bank so that you can make a big purchase. Financing is a means of obtaining money, then paying the loan back in a specified time period for a set monthly amount. Upon approval, the bank will pay the merchant the total cost for what you are buying and they (the bank) will send you a bill each month.

2. In your own words, describe what a Credit Report is.
A Credit Report is a detailed record of your payment history with lenders and is an indicator that reflects how well or badly you manage your financial matters.

3. What are the names of the three major credit bureaus in the US?
Experian, TransUnion, and Equifax.

4. What is the main function of Credit Bureaus?

A Credit Bureau is an agency that gathers information on how consumers use their credit and how they pay back what they borrowed. Credit bureaus collect your information from as many financial transactions or inquiries as they can. Then they sell access to that information to anyone who has a legally-recognized and legitimate reason to use it.

5. What are the consequences of having a low Credit Rating (FICO score)?
With a low credit score, you may not get financing and if you do, you may be offered high interest rates that can cost hundreds of thousands of dollars down the line.

6. What is the name of the act that states that information on your Credit Report must be complete and accurate?
Fair Credit Reporting Act

7. What can you do to dispute wrong information on your credit report?
Many inaccuracies can be fixed by sending a certified letter to the three major Credit Reporting agencies, setting forth all of the facts and any written proof that the debt is reported inaccurately. You should copy this letter to the creditor or debt collector whose name appears on the bottom of your reports.

8. How is a FICO score calculated?
A FICO (Fair Isaac Corporation) Score is calculated based on the information contained in your Credit Report. The numbers are generated by a computer program that runs through your Report. It looks for patterns, characteristics, and red flags in your credit history. Based on what the program finds, it spits out a score. Scores typically range from 350 to 850 with higher numbers being much better. The more negative information you have on your Credit Report, the lower your score will be.

9. Name the five areas that make up a credit score.
>Payment History (35%)
>Amount OWED Compared To Available Credit (30%)
>Length of Credit HISTORY (15%)
>Inquiries and New Debt (10%)
>Type of Debt (10%)

10. Explain what an Interest Rate is.
An interest rate is a percentage of the money borrowed that you must pay on top of the money that you must pay back.

11. An excellent FICO credit score is:
Answers may vary, but anywhere between <u>700-850</u> is good.

12. An "R1" rating on your report means.
R1 means that you pay your bills on time every month, which is within 30 days.

13. Your "Payment History" makes up what percentage of your credit report?
>35%

14. The length of your credit history makes up what percentage of your credit report?
>15%

15. The total amount owed makes up what percentage of your credit report?
>30%

16. Name at least five things you can do to keep your credit in good standing.

- ✓ Pay all your bills on time.
- ✓ Always pay the minimum payment due.
- ✓ Pay extra on the minimum payment.
- ✓ Always keep a balance.
- ✓ Don't max out your credit cards or go over your
- ✓ limit.
- ✓ Minimize outstanding debt.
- ✓ Refrain from applying for credit unnecessarily.
- ✓ Keep old accounts open.
- ✓ Review your Credit Report frequently.
- ✓ Go Automatic.

17. Name at least five things that make your Credit Record bad.
Answers may include any of the following:
- ✓ Making late payments
- ✓ NEGLECTING TO pay at all
- ✓ Letting an account get charged off
- ✓ Letting an account get sent to collections
- ✓ Defaulting on a loan
- ✓ Filing bankruptcy (More on this later)
- ✓ Foreclosure (More on this later)

- ✓ Getting a judgment against you
- ✓ High credit card balances
- ✓ Maxed out credit cards
- ✓ Closing credit cards that still have balances
- ✓ Closing old credit cards
- ✓ Applying for several credit cards or loans
- ✓ Having only credit cards or only loans
- ✓ Co-signing for Someone

18. In your opinion, what was the purpose of the Credit Card accountability Responsibility and Disclosure Act?

Answers will vary

19. Name at least three components of the Credit Card accountability Responsibility and Disclosure Act?

- ✓ Must Have a Note From Your Parents
- ✓ No More Free Giveaways for Filling out an Application
- ✓ No More Secret Deals
- ✓ No Release of Credit Report for Students Under 21
- ✓ No More Over-The-Limit Fees
- ✓ Late Fees Capped

20. On the lines below, write at least three things that you are going to start doing immediately to increase your credit score.

Answers will vary

7
Managing Your Money Strategically

Two Cents worth:
Don't make money your goal. Instead pursue the things you love doing and the money will come to you by default.

Dr. Mia Y. Merritt

DATE _____

1. Name two accounts that banks sometimes offer with no monthly fee.

    I. _____

    II. _____

2. Name two companies that sell checkbooks at discounted prices.

    I. _____

    II. _____

3. The key to becoming wealthy is not how much money you make, but how much of it you _____.

4. A budget is also called a _____.

5. A distinct account or fund that everyone should have in case of a rainy day is called a(n). _____.

6. In order to determine if you are in debt, the first thing you should do is what?

_____

_____

_____

7. An ideal Emergency Fund amount should have how many months of household expenses in it? _____

8. What typically keeps most people in debt? _____

_____

_____

_____

9. Name at least two things that one should do to keep their Emergency Fund growing.

   I. _____

   II. _____

10. After you receive your paycheck, the IRS has already taken out taxes. What is the next thing you should do with at least 10 % of your money?

_____

_____

_____

11. What are the three baskets a person should have money in?

   I. _____

   II. _____

   III. _____

12. What is the purpose of an Emergency Fund?

_____

_____

13. In your own words, explain Emotional Spending.

_____

_____

14. What do you think you will discover if you kept a record of everything you bought for one month and then added up the total?

_____

_____

15. If you find that you are wasting a lot of money, would you be willing to curtail your spending? ___ yes ___ no. Why or why not?

_____

_____

_____

16. It is fine to use credit cards for food and toiletries. _____

17. All credit cards have the same Annual Percentage Rate. _____

18. A credit card should ideally be used for emergency purposes only. _____

19. All credit cards have an annual fee. _____

20. Credit cards and debit cards are basically the same thing. _____

21. One should wait until they get older to save for retirement. _____

RETIREMENT

22. When should you begin saving for your retirement? _____

23. Name two popular Retirement Plans that companies, organizations, or businesses offer to their employees. _____ _____

24. What is an incentive that some organizations do for their employees when they contribute to their Retirement Plan? _____

25. If you leave a company that offered a Retirement Plan and begin working at a company that does not offer the plan, what can you do with the money you contributed from your previous employer? _____

26. What is a Roth IRA?

   _____
   _____
   _____

27. Who can have a Roth?

   _____
   _____
   _____

28. What is the maximum amount of money a person can put into a Roth? _____

29. What is the maximum amount of money a person over 50 years of age can put into a Roth IRA? _____

30. What is the main difference between a Roth and a traditional 401K or 403B?

   _____
   _____
   _____

TAXES

Dr. Mia Y. Merritt, M&M Motivating
Life After High School: Valuable Life Skills for the Goal-Oriented Achiever!

31. When do you pay taxes on a Roth IRA? _____

_____

_____

_____

32. Do you think it is better to pay more federal withholding during the year (to get a refund) or to pay less during the year (to bring more money home)? Explain your answer.

_____

_____

_____

33. What is the name of the form that determines how much money will be taken out of your check when you are hired at a job? _____

34. What does FICA stand for? _____

35. What does FICA tax pay when it is deducted from your paycheck?

_____

_____

36. What is the percentage of FICA that is taken out of everyone's paycheck? _____

37. Broken down, what is the individual percentage of social security and Medicare that makes the total FICA tax?

      SS: _____

      Medicare: _____

38. Do you have medical insurance? ___ yes ___ no

39. If not, what will you do if you require medical attention? _____

_____

_____

_____

40. How do you plan on getting medical insurance in the near future if you do not have any?

_____

_____

_____

41. Do you have life insurance? ___yes ___ no

       If yes, do you know which of the two kinds it is (term or whole life)?
          ___yes ___ no

42. What is the difference between the two different kinds of life insurance?

_____

_____

_____

43. Analyzing your personal situation, which type of insurance is best for you?

    ___ Whole Life Insurance
    ___ Term Life Insurance

44. Do you have enough life insurance to bury you and pay off all your debt? ___yes ___ no

45. PART B:
If you are 21 years or older, complete the exercises that follow:

    List all your credit cards on the next page:

CREDIT CARD	BALANCE OWED	CREDIT LIMIT	APR%	TARGET DATE TO PAY IT OFF

Based on the table above, how much money do you owe in credit card debt? $ _____

In helping you to develop a Spending Plan, complete the following exercises:

My annual (gross) income is: _____ My net income (every paycheck) is _____ . My federal withholding amount is _____ . My FICA/Social Security amount is _____ .

List all of your payroll deductions and amounts below:

DEDUCTION	AMOUNT	TOTAL
Ex: Medical Ins.	$ 153.00	$153.00
United Way	$15.00	$168.00

According to your figures above, what is the total amount of your deductions including taxes?

_____

Review all of your deductions above and see if there are any that you can cut out. List them below:

_____ _____ _____

_____ _____ _____

On the lines below, make a list all of your household expenses.

Example:	AMOUNT	TOTAL
Rent	$650.00	$650.00
Car Payment	$300.00	$950.00

My total monthly expenses are: _____.

As I review my income and calculate my monthly expenses, I am (choose one):

___ in the positive with _____ dollars left over each month.

___ in the negative by _____ dollars each month.

If you have money left over each month, do you see where the extra money (surplus) goes?

___ yes   ___ no.   Explain

_____

_____

(The exercise on page 82 can help reveal where the money goes.)

If you do not have money left over, what are you prepared to do to change this?

_____

_____

Based on what you have learned, where should your extra money be going?

_____

_____

If you are in the negative each month, what are you prepared to do to get out of the negative?

Part C: FINANCIAL EXERCISE:
For one month, keep a record of everything you spend. Do this for 30 consecutive days. If you start on April 15th, then you must review your findings on May 15th. This includes everything paid out of your net income (rent, car payment, utilities, clothes, food, etc.) This does not include deductions that are already taken out.

Date to begin: _____

Turn the Page

You are given extra lines for the days that you buy more than one or two things in a day. (You may buy a new shirt, then gas, then a meal at Red Lobster. You may then pick up a prescription at the local drug store – all in the same day. You must keep track of each of these things and put them in your log.

DATE	STORE	PURCHASE	AMOUNT	TOTAL

DATE	STORE	PURCHASE	AMOUNT	TOTAL

Dr. Mia Y. Merritt, M&M Motivating
Life After High School: Valuable Life Skills for the Goal-Oriented Achiever!

Self-check
- I will analyze my monthly income v/s my outgoing expenses to see if I have money left over each month.
- I will make a log of *everything* I spend for one month so I can "see" where my money goes.
- I will begin at once to put money into an Emergency Fund even if I have to start small.
- I will begin at once to put money into my Retirement Fund even if I have to start small.
- I will analyze all my deductions to see if there are any I can cut out.
- I will not use my credit cards unless it is an emergency.
- I will get the percentage rate of all my credit cards and try to negotiate a better rate if necessary.
- I begin to pay down all my balances to less than 50% starting with the smallest balance first.
- I will shop for medical insurance as soon as possible if I do not have any.

Time to Reflect

Now that you have learned the secret to building wealth, do you feel that you are better prepared to secure a solid financial future for yourself? Explain how your spending habits will change as a result of the information you learned from the chapter on *Managing Your Money Strategically*.

Chapter 7 Answer Key

1. Name two accounts that banks sometimes offer for free.
   Checking and savings accounts

2. Name two companies that sell checkbooks at discounted prices.
   Checks in the mail and checks unlimited

3. The key to becoming wealthy is not how much money you make, but how much of it you:
   SPEND OR SAVE.

4. A budget is also called a:
   SPENDING PLAN

5. An account that everyone should have in case of a rainy day is called a(n).

   EMERGENCY PLAN

6. In order to determine if you are in debt, the first thing you should do is what?
   Answers will vary, but may include:

   Add up your monthly bills
   Do a Spending Plan (budget)

7. An ideal Emergency Fund amount should have how many months of household expenses in it?
   Between 3-6 months

8. What typically keeps most people in debt?
   Answers will vary, but may include:

   Frivolous spending
   Irresponsible use of credit cards
   Trying to keep up with the Jones
   Buying this you can't afford
   Not saving/investing

9. Name at least two things that one should do to keep money into their Emergency Fund.
   Make it an automatic withdrawal
   Have a set amount taken out frequently

10. After you receive your paycheck, the IRS has already taken out taxes. What is the next thing you should do with at least 10 % of your money?

Pay yourself first.
Put a certain amount in your emergency fund

11. Typically, what are the three baskets a person should have money in?
    Dream Basket
    Retirement Basket
    Emergency Fund Basket

12. What is the purpose of an Emergency Fund?
    The emergency fund protects you and your family against the unexpected (job loss, medical emergency, death of a loved one, emergency home repairs, etc).

13. In your own words, explain Emotional Spending.
    When people buy things they really do not need or want because they think it will make them feel better. Some people resort to this when they are feeling depressed, have anxiety, are frustrated, stressed, bored, under-appreciated, are feeling inferior, etc.

14. What do you think you will discover if you kept a record of everything you bought for one month and then added up the total?
    There is no right or wrong answer

15. If you find that you are wasting a lot of money, would you be willing to curtail your spending? ___ yes ___ no. why or why not?
    There is no right or wrong answer

16. It is fine to use credit cards for food or toiletries.

    False

17. All credit cards have the same Annual Percentage Rate.

    False

18. A credit card should ideally be used for emergency purposes only.

    True

19. Not all credit cards have an annual fee.

    True

20. Credit cards and debit cards are basically the same thing.

    False

21. What is the importance of saving for retirement as soon as possible?

    Because of the power of compounding. The earlier you begin, the more money you will have in your account when its time for retirement.

22. When should you begin saving for your retirement?
    As soon as you begin working on a permanent full-time job.

23. Name two popular Retirement Plans that companies, organizations or businesses offer to their employees. **401k and 403b**

24. What is an incentive that some organizations do for their employees when they contribute to their Retirement Plan?
Many of them will match part of all of your retirement contributions.

25. If you leave a company that offered a Retirement Plan and begin working at a company that does not offer the plan, what can you do with the money you contributed from your previous employer?
Do a 401k roller over into a traditional IRA

26. What is a Roth IRA?
A Roth IRA is also a retirement plan that can invest in securities, usually common stocks or mutual funds (although other investments, including derivatives, notes, certificates of deposit, and real estate are possible).

27. Who can have a Roth?
Anyone at any age can open a Roth IRA account. Minors may even establish and contribute to a Roth IRA provided the minor has verifiable income.

28. What is the maximum amount of money a person can put into a Roth? $5,000
If you are under the age of 50, you may contribute up to $5,000 a year. If you are over 50, you can contribute up to $6,000 a year under the catch-up provision.

29. What is the maximum amount of money a person over 50 years of age can put into a Roth IRA? **$6,000**

30. What is the main difference between a Roth and a traditional 401K or 403B?

Roth IRA	Traditional IRA
Individuals of all ages can open up a Roth	Must be at least 18 to open up a retirement account
Pay no taxes when you withdraw money at age 59 ½	Pay taxes on the money you withdraw
Contributions can be withdrawn at any time, tax free.	Contributions can be withdrawn at any time, tax free.
Pay a 10% penalty for early withdrawal	Pay a 10% penalty for early withdrawal
There are no required minimum distributions	You have to withdraw a minimum amount
Contributions are NOT tax deductible	Contributions ARE tax deductible
Assets can be passed onto beneficiaries after death.	Assets can be passed onto beneficiaries after death.

31. How is federal withholding tax calculated with a Roth?
You pay as you contribute. Pay no taxes when you withdraw money at age 59 ½

32. Do you think it is better to pay more federal withholding during the year (to get a refund) or to pay less during the year (to bring more money home)? Explain your answer. **There is no right or wrong answer**

33. What is the name of the form that determines how much money will be taken out of your check when you are hired at a job? **W4**

34. What does FICA stand for?
Federal Insurance Contribution Act

35. What does FICA tax pay when it is deducted from your paycheck?
Social Security and Medicare

36. What is the percentage of FICA that is taken out of everyone's paycheck? **7.65%**

37. Broken down, what is the individual percentage of social security and Medicare that makes the total FICA tax?

    SS: 6.2%
    Medicare: 1.45%

38. Do you have medical insurance? **Answers will vary**

39. If not, what will you do if you require medical attention? **Answers will vary**

40. How do you plan on getting medical insurance in the near future if you do not have
Answers will vary

41. Do you have life insurance? If yes, do you know which of the two kinds it is (term or whole life)? **Answers will vary**

42. What is the difference between the two different kinds of life insurance?
The main difference between the two is the period of time that the insurance policy is valid, either for a short "term" or for your "whole" life.

43. Analyzing your personal situation, which type of insurance is best for you?
    Answers will vary

44. Do you have enough life insurance to bury you and pay off all your debt?
    Answers will vary

45. PART B:
If you are 21 years or older, complete the exercises below:
    Answers will vary

8
Sex, Diseases & Responsibilities

Two Cents worth:

In our culture, talking about sex is embarrassing, and talking about diseases that come from sex is even more so. And because people don't talk about it, there's not a good way for teenagers to learn about it.

Julie Downs

DATE _____

1. Based on what you have learned, what is the best method of protection to use against sexually transmitted diseases? _____

2. What is the best method for storing condoms and why?

_____
_____
_____

3. In your own words, explain what a Sexually Transmitted Disease (STD) is.

_____
_____
_____

4. Name the five most common STDs in America.

    I. _____

    II. _____

    III. _____

IV. _____

V. _____

5. Which STD gives a whitish, greenish or yellow discharge from the penis or vagina after nine days?

_____

_____

_____

6. Is the above disease curable? __ yes ___ no. If yes, explain how it is cured. If no, explain how it is treated.

_____

_____

_____

7. Which STD infects the cervix in women and the penile urethra in men? This STD can also lead to non-gonococcal-urethritis (NGU) in men and Pelvic Inflammatory Disease (PID) in women leading to Cervical Cancer.

_____

8. Is the above disease curable? __ yes ___ no. If yes, explain how it is cured. If no, explain how it is treated.

_____

_____

_____

9. Which STD causes hard, red, painless sores which disappear after six weeks and returns for stage two, which brings rashes, swollen lymph glands, sore throat, weight loss, headache and/or hair loss?

_____

10. Is the above disease curable? __ yes ___ no. If yes, explain how it is cured. If no, explain how it is treated.

_____

_____

_____

11. Which STD causes small warts or growths on the genital organs?

_____

12. Is the above disease curable? __ yes ___ no? If yes, explain how it is cured. . If no, explain how it is treated.

_____

_____

_____

13. What does HIV stand for?

_____

14. What does AIDS stand for?

_____

15. What is the difference between HIV and AIDS?

_____

_____

_____

16. Is there a cure for HIV? __ yes ___ no Is there a cure for AIDS? __ yes ___ no If yes, explain how they are cured. If no, explain how they are treated.

Dr. Mia Y. Merritt, M&M Motivating
Life After High School: Valuable Life Skills for the Goal-Oriented Achiever!

17. What are some of the initial symptoms of HIV?

18. HIV infected people may seem outwardly healthy for how many years or longer?

19. What system of the body is being attacked in an HIV infected person?

20. What treatment is used with HIV infected individuals?

21. In your own words, explain what happens after the HIV deficiency becomes so bad that the body is no longer able to fight back infections and other diseases?

22. How does HIV enter the body?

23. Which particular cell does HIV target? _____

24. What does this particular cell normally do for the body?

25. The main purpose of the HIV Virus in the body is to do what?

26. What does the *syndrome* part of the AIDS (the "S") actually mean?

27. What is the best method of HIV prevention?

28. Explain what a Viral Infection is.

29. Explain what a Bacterial Infection is.

30. What is the difference between a Viral and Bacterial Infection?

TRUE/FALSE

31. There are only a few methods of birth control. _____

32. A girl can not get pregnant if it is her first time having sex. _____

33. You can not get an STD from oral sex. _____

34. Having sex and making love technically mean the same thing. _____

35. Spermicides kills sperm and stops it from traveling up into the cervix. _____

36. The male condom can break if it is old or has been stored in heated places. _____

37. The male and female condom should be used at the same time. _____

38. Birth control pills prevent the release of an egg during the monthly cycle. _____

39. If a girl misses taking a birth control pill for two consecutive days, she can get pregnant. _____

40. The withdrawal method can be used by all boys and men. _____

41. In your own words, explain abstinence.

_____

_____

_____

42. In your own words, explain casual sex and whether or not you think it is okay to engage in casual sex.

_____

_____

_____

43. What does it mean to be promiscuous?

_____

_____

_____

44. Do you think it is okay to be promiscuous if you use protection with the partners? Explain.

_____

_____

_____

45. In your own words, explain sex transmutation.

_____

_____

_____

_____

Promiscuous	**a.** when a man pulls his penis out of the vagina before ejaculation
Bacteria	**b.** require living hosts, such as people, plants or animals to multiply otherwise, they can not survive.
Condom	**c.** chemical agents that kill sperm and stops it from traveling up into the cervix.
Abstinence	**d.** a choice to refrain from sexual activity
Viruses	**e.** is put on a man's penis while the penis is erect.
Orgasm	**f.** having many random or casual sex partners on a frequent basis.
Withdrawal	**g.** single-celled microorganisms that live in extremes of cold or heat, while others make their home in the intestines of individuals
Spermicides	**h.** the release of tension that follows sexual activity. It is a feeling of ecstasy that lasts for about 15 seconds

Promiscuous ___

Bacteria ___

Condom ___

Abstinence ___

Viruses ___

Orgasm ___

Withdrawal ___

Spermicides ___

Self-check
- ✓ I will make an appointment for my annual physical if I have not already done so.
- ✓ If I choose to be sexually active, I will have only one).
- ✓ I will use the method of protection that is best for me.
- ✓ I will not take genital discharges, rashes, or sores lightly, but will seek medical attention right away.
- ✓ I will stay abreast of important information pertaining to sex, responsibilities and the importance of safe sex.

Time to Reflect

Now that you have learned about the dangers of having unprotected sex and the types of damage that STDs can have on the body, what are you prepared to do to "stay" clear of these detrimental, negative, life-changing diseases? How do you feel about what you have learned?

Chapter 8 Answer Key

1. Based on what you have learned, what is the best method of protection to use against sexually transmitted diseases?

Abstinence

2. What is the worst method for storing condoms and why?
It is not smart to use a condom that has been stored in your back pocket, purse, wallet, or glove compartment of your car.

3. In your own words, explain what a Sexually Transmitted Disease (STD) is.
Answers will vary, but may include diseases that you get from having unprotected sex.

4. Name the five most common STDs in America.

Syphilis
Chlamydia
Gonorrhea
Human Papillomavirus -HPV
Human Immunodeficiency Virus -HIV

5. Which STD gives a whitish, greenish or yellow discharge from the penis or vagina after nine days?

Chlamydia

6. Is the above disease curable? If yes, explain how it is cured. If no, explain how it is treated.
Yes Chlamydia is curable. Chlamydia is treated with antibiotics such as azithromycin (Zithromax), taken as a pill.

7. Which STD infects the cervix in women and the penile urethra in men? This STD can also lead to non-gonococcal-urethritis (NGU) in men and Pelvic Inflammatory Disease in women leading to Cervical Cancer.

Chlamydia

8. Is the above disease curable. If yes, explain how it is cured. If no, explain how it is treated.
Yes Chlamydia is curable. Chlamydia is treated with antibiotics such as azithromycin (Zithromax), taken as a pill.

9. Which STD causes hard, red, painless sores which disappear after six weeks and returns for stage two, which brings rashes, swollen lymph glands, sore throat, weight loss, headache and/or hair loss? **Syphilis**

10 Is the above disease curable? __ yes ___ no. If yes, explain how it is cured. . If no, explain how it is treated.

Yes, Syphilis is curable. It is treated with large doses of penicillin or other antibiotics for as long as needed until the person is cured. It is important not to have sex until one is completely cured.

11. Which STD causes small warts or growths on the genital organs?
Human Papillomavirus -HPV

12. Is the above disease curable? __ yes ___ no? If yes, explain how it is cured. . If no, explain how it is treated.
There is no cure for HPV, but genital warts that are visible do require medical treatment. They can be removed by directly applied medications, laser treatment, freezing, electrical cauterization, or surgery.

13. What does HIV stand for? **Human Immunodeficiency**

14. What does AIDS stand for? **Acquired Immune Deficiency Syndrome**

15. What is the difference between HIV and AIDS?
When a person with an HIV-weakened immune system comes down with one or more of these rare opportunistic infections, or has a T cell count below 200 or 14%, that person may be diagnosed by a doctor as having AIDS. The syndrome part means that AIDS is not a single disease but a collection of diseases.

16. Is there a cure for HIV? __ yes ___ no   Is there a cure for AIDS? __ yes ___ no   If yes, explain how they are cured. If no, explain how they are treated.
At this time, there is no cure for the HIV infection and no cure for AIDS. However, various treatments are now available that can slow down the progression of the disease and prolong life. Currently, most people with HIV are treated with a combination of drugs known as Highly Active Anti-retroviral Therapy, or HAART.

17. What are some of the initial symptoms of HIV?
At first, an infected person may not develop any symptoms at all or only some temporary flu-like symptoms such as fever, a sore throat, diarrhea, swollen lymph nodes, and pain in various parts of the body. Often, these symptoms are not taken seriously, and thus the infection may not be recognized for what it is. This first stage of the disease is called "primary HIV infection" or "acute HIV infection".

18. HIV infected people may seem outwardly healthy for how many years or longer?
10 years or longer

19. What system of the body is being attacked in an HIV infected person?
Immune system

20. What treatment is used with HIV infected individuals?
Various treatments are now available that can slow down the progression of the disease and prolong life. Currently, most people with HIV are treated with a combination of drugs known as Highly Active Anti-retroviral Therapy, or HAART.

21. In your own words, explain what happens after the HIV deficiency becomes so bad that the body is no longer able to fight back infections and other diseases?

Answers may vary

22. How does HIV enter the body?

HIV enters the body through some small cut or break in the skin or mucous membranes. This can occur during vaginal, oral, or anal sexual contact.

23. Which particular cell does HIV target?

HIV is best known for targeting the "T" cells of the immune system.

24. What does this particular cell normally do for the body?

The main job of T-cells is to fight off infections. There are a number of different types of T-cells that act in many ways to identify, directly attack and destroy infectious agents. Along with other white blood cells, they play a major role in the immune system, which guards the body against infection.

25. The main purpose of the HIV Virus in the body is to do what?

Like all viruses, the HIV is only interested in one thing: reproducing itself.

26. What does the syndrome part of the AIDS (the S) actually mean?

The syndrome part means that AIDS is not a single disease but a collection of diseases.

27. What is the best method of HIV prevention?

Abstinence

28. Explain what a viral infection is.

Viruses require living hosts, such as people, plants or animals to multiply, otherwise they can not survive. When a virus enters your body, it invades some of your cells and takes over the cell machinery, redirecting it to produce the virus.

29. Explain what a bacterial infection is.

Bacteria are single-celled microorganisms that thrive in many different types of environments. Some live in extremes of cold or heat, while others make their home in the intestines of individuals, where they help digest food.

30. What is the difference between the two?

Perhaps the most important distinction between bacteria and viruses is that antibiotic drugs usually kill bacteria, but they are not effective against viruses. In some cases, it may be difficult to determine whether bacteria or a virus is causing your symptoms.

31. There are only a few methods of birth control. **False**

32. A girl can not get pregnant if it is her first time having sex. **False**

33. You can not get an STD from oral sex. **False**

34. Having sex and making love technically mean the same thing. **True**

35. Spermicides kills sperm and stops it from traveling up into the cervix. **True**

36. The male condom can break if it is old or has been stored in heated places. **True**

37. The male and female condom should be used at the same time. **False**

38. Birth control pills prevent the release of an egg during the monthly cycle. **True**

39. If a girl misses taking a birth control pill for two days, she can get pregnant. **True**

40. The withdrawal method can be used by all boys and men. **False**

41. In your own words, explain abstinence.
> **Answers will vary**

42. In your own words, explain casual sex and whether or not you think it is okay to engage in casual sex.
> **Answers will vary**

43. What does it mean to be promiscuous?
Having many random or casual sex partners. There really is not much of a difference between casual sex and promiscuity. The only difference is in frequency.

44. Do you think it is okay to be promiscuous if you use protection with the partners?
> **Answers will vary**

45. In your own words, explain sex transmutation.
> **Answers will vary**

9
Drugs & Alcohol

Two Cents worth:

In the 1960s, people took acid to make the world weird. Now the world is weird, and people take Prozac to make it normal.

Author Unknown

DATE _____

1. Based on what you have learned about drug addicts and alcoholics, why do people take these substances?

   _____

   _____

   _____

2. What typically happens after a person comes down off of the high that drugs and alcohol give?

   _____

   _____

   _____

3. Name the five most common drugs used in America today.

   I. _____

   II. _____

   III. _____

   IV. _____

Dr. Mia Y. Merritt, M&M Motivating
Life After High School: Valuable Life Skills for the Goal-Oriented Achiever!

V. _____

4. In your own words explain addiction.

_____

_____

_____

5. Based on what you have learned, is alcohol a stimulant or a depressant?

   ___ stimulant   ___ depressant

6. What are some of the consequences of becoming an addict?

_____

_____

_____

7. Are addicts always visibly obvious? Explain.

_____

_____

_____

Based on your memory, answer the questions below on the following drugs.

MARIJUANA

8. What is marijuana made from?

_____

_____

_____

9. What is the made ingredient called in marijuana that makes it potent?

_____

10. After taking the drug, how does it make a user feel?

_____

_____

_____

11. Name the long term effects of taking marijuana.

_____

_____

_____

12. What are two street names for marijuana?

_____   _____

13. What are some addictive effects of marijuana?

_____

_____

_____

14. Does a person develop a tolerance for marijuana? ___ Yes ___ no

AMPHETAMINES

15. Explain what an amphetamine is?

_____

_____

_____

16. What were amphetamines originally made for?

_____

_____

17. After taking the drug, how does it make a user feel?

18. Name at least two long term effects of taking amphetamines.

19. What are some addictive effects of amphetamines?

20. What are two street names for amphetamines?

COCAINE

21. What is cocaine made from?

22. How is cocaine usually prepared?

23. After taking the drug, how does it make a user feel?

_____
_____
_____

24. How long does the high normally last.

_____

25. Does a person develop a tolerance for cocaine?

___ yes ___ no

26. What are two street names for cocaine?

_____   _____

27. Name at least two long term effects of taking cocaine.

    I. _____

    II. _____

28. What are some physical addictive effects of taking cocaine?

_____
_____
_____

CRACK

29. Explain what crack is?

_____
_____
_____

30. Crack is a form of what? _____

31. How is crack usually prepared?

32. Name two ingredients that crack is cooked with and why is it called "crack"?

33. Crack is usually smoked in what? _____

      Does a person develop a tolerance for crack cocaine? __yes __ no

34. About how long does it take for crack to get into the bloodstream?

35. After taking the drug, how does it make a user feel?

36. How long does the high normally last? _____

37. What are the long term effects of taking crack?

38. What are some addictive effects of taking crack?

39. Which high last longer, crack or cocaine?

                         ___ crack   ___ cocaine

OPIATES

40. Based on what you have learned, what are opiates?

41. Name three common opiates usually referred to by their medical name.

       I. _____

      II. _____

    III. _____

42. How do opiates usually make users feel?

43. What is heroin?

44. How is heroin prepared?

45. What is the main ingredient in heroin? _____

46. In what common ways is heroin taken?

47. How does is make a user feel after they have taken the drug?

48. What happens to a user after the drug wears off? What do they experience?

49. What are the long-term effects of heroin?

50. Does a person develop a tolerance for heroin?

51. What is the best way for a user to detoxify from heroin?

_____

_____

ALCOHOL

52. What is alcohol made from?

_____

_____

_____

53. What does alcohol do to the body after it is taken?

_____

_____

_____

54. Alcohol is very high in what? _____

55. What does **DUI** stand for and what does it mean?

_____

_____

_____

56. What does **DWI** stand for and what does it mean?

_____

_____

_____

57. What are the four parts to alcoholism?

    1. _____

    2. _____

3. _____

4. _____

58. What is a hangover?

_____

_____

_____

59. What does being "present" mean?

_____

_____

_____

60. What does drinking in *moderation* mean?

_____

_____

_____

61. In what ways are you going to show responsibility when drinking?

_____

_____

_____

62. What is counterfeit happiness?

_____

_____

_____

63. What can you do to deal with your problems instead of drinking or using drugs?

_____

_____

_____

Time to Reflect

Men, women, and children die in drunk driving accidents every day because someone thought they were sober enough to drive when they had been drinking. Additionally, others have died by drug overdoses while searching for a temporary high that gives them a brief escape from reality. Why do you think that some things like drugs and alcohol can make people feel so good (temporary) and then make them feel so bad down the line and eventually destroy lives? Explain.

Self-check
- ✓ Before going out, I will decide before hand how many drinks I will have.
- ✓ I will not overindulge in any alcoholic beverage as a means of having a good time.
- ✓ If I drink, I will not drive.
- ✓ I will not allow a friend or family member to drink and drive.
- ✓ I will stay clear of drugs as a means of temporary happiness and joy, but will seek inner joy and peace.
- ✓ I will not take drugs at all!
- ✓ I will seek to help a family member or friend that may be struggling with drugs or alcohol.
- ✓ Before making a decision that could impact my future, I will stop, focus on my goals and refrain from making a negative choice.

Chapter 9 Answer Key

1. Based on what you have learned about drug addicts and alcoholics, why do people take these substances?

People who take drugs and alcohol, do so because they like how the substances make them feel. These substances cause temporary changes in the brain that produce a high. Individuals tend to relax and experience a slightly altered state of consciousness while under the influence of drugs or alcohol. In many cases, people do drugs because they are trying to escape from the problems and issues in their life.

2. What typically happens after a person comes down off of the high that drugs and alcohol give?

    After the drug wears off, users feel severe depression, exhaustion and irritability.

3. Name the five most common drugs used in America today.

    Answers may vary, but may include:
    - **Marijuana**
    - **Amphetamines**
    - **Cocaine**
    - *Crack – a form of Cocaine*
    - **Methamphetamines / Ecstasy**
    - **Opiates**
    - **Heroin**
    - **Codeine**

4. In your own words explain addiction.

    Needing drugs or alcohol regardless of the effects it may have on the body

5. Based on what you have learned, is alcohol a stimulant or a depressant?

    Depressant

6. What are some of the consequences of becoming an addict?

    Answers may vary

7. Are addicts always visibly obvious? Explain.

Addicts are not always easy to spot because they are not always obvious drunks or junkies. They could be people who have a drink everyday, even though they may never get drunk. They could also be people who use drugs everyday, but still manage to work and live their lives effectively while maintaining a good "buzz".

8. What is marijuana made from?

It is a dry, shredded green and brown mix of flowers, stems, seeds, and leaves derived from the hemp plant Cannabis sativa.

9. What is the made ingredient called in marijuana that makes it potent?
The main mind-altering ingredient in marijuana is THC, but more than 400 other chemicals also are in the plant.

10. After taking the drug, how does it make a user feel?
Some individuals feel very calm, some laugh a lot, some get very hungry and some just feel a sense of great relaxation.

11. Name the long term effects of taking marijuana.
The drug can impair or reduce short-term memory, alter sense of time, and reduce ability to do things which require concentration, swift reactions, and coordination, such as driving a car or operating machinery.

12. What are two street names for marijuana? Answers may include
   Grass, pot, weed

13. What are some addictive effects of marijuana?
Can significantly increases the chance of lung cancer, inflammation, and infection. Long-term marijuana abuse can lead to addiction.

14. Does a person develop a tolerance for marijuana?

Those who try and detoxify themselves from the drug, report extreme irritability, enormous sleeplessness, decreased appetite, major anxiety, and a massive craving for the drug, all of which makes it difficult to quit.

15. Explain what an amphetamine is?
Amphetamines are a white powder.

16. What was amphetamines originally made for?
medication for asthma patients

17. After taking the drug, how does it make a user feel?
People under the influence of this drug report having an increase in energy, cheerfulness, and great confidence. The drug reduces the need for sleep and suppresses the appetite.

18. Name at least two long term effects of taking amphetamines.
Long term user may experience delusions, hallucinations, and paranoia, which may develop into full-blown paranoid psychosis.

19. What are some addictive effects of amphetamines?
Amphetamines are psychologically addictive. Users who try to stop, report that they experience a mixture of mood swings such as aggression, anxiety, and intense cravings for the drugs. Amphetamine users also report a need to use more and more of the drug to obtain the same effect for every succeeding "high", and this places an

extra burden on the body and may cause delusions, hallucinations, and paranoia, which may develop into full-blown paranoid psychosis.**

20. What are two street names for amphetamines? **Answers may vary, but may include Speed, Whizz, Billy and Sulph.**

21. What is cocaine made from?
Cocaine is produced as a white chunky powder and is derived from coco leaves (Erythroxylon coca).

22. How is cocaine usually prepared?
It is sold most often in aluminum foil, plastic or paper packets, or small vials. Cocaine is usually chopped into a fine powder with a razor blade on a small mirror or some other hard surface, arranged into small rows called "lines," then inhaled (or "snorted") through the nose with a short straw or rolled up paper money. It can also be injected into the blood stream.

23. After taking the drug, how does it make a user feel?
An intense feeling of euphoria and a burst of energy is reported to occur after snorting cocaine.

24. How long does the high normally last.
The high lasts between 15-30 minutes.

25. Does a person develop a tolerance for cocaine?
Cocaine users reportedly do not develop a tolerance for it, so the amount inhaled or injected usually always gives them the desired high without having to be increased with additional use, but the temptation to increase the dose to intensify the effect of the drug is reportedly very high.

26. What are two street names for cocaine?
Rock, Charlie, Coke and Snarfy

Name at least two long term effects of taking cocaine.
Irritability, restlessness and paranoia in prolonged use.

27. What are some physical addictive effects of taking cocaine?
Prolonged use of cocaine damages the membrane of the nose and causes a weakening of the septum and eventually total disintegration of the septum may occur.

28. Explain what crack is?
Crack is made from cocaine in a process called freebasing, in which cocaine powder is cooked with ammonia or baking soda to create crystals or rocks, chips, or chunks that are smoked and produces a longer high. It also is more readily absorbed through the lungs.

29. Crack is a form of what?
Crack is a more potent form of cocaine

30. How is crack usually prepared?

31. Name two ingredients that crack is cooked with.
ammonia or baking soda

Why is it called "crack"?
The term crack refers to the crackling sound that is heard when the mixture is smoked. Crack is usually smoked in a pipe.

32. Crack is usually smoked in what?
A pipe

33. About how long does it take for crack to get into the bloodstream?
The vapors of the crack are absorbed through the lungs into the bloodstream and transported to the brain within 10-15 seconds!

34. After taking the drug, how does it make a user feel?
An intense feeling of euphoria and a burst of energy is reported to occur after snorting cocaine.

35. How long does the high normally last?
less than 15 minutes.

36. What are the long term effects of taking crack?
Crack addicts must have more and more crack to sustain their high and to avoid the intense "crash" or heavy depression that follows their binges. They become physically and psychologically dependent on this drug, which leads to addiction. This is often a result of only few doses of the drug taken within a few days.

37. What are some addictive effects of taking crack?
They become physically and psychologically dependent on this drug, which leads to addiction.

38. Which high last longer, crack or cocaine?
Cocaine

39. Based on what you have learned, what are opiates?
Opiates are drugs that take away pain, but in the process of eliminating pain, they give a great feeling of euphoria or "high". Opiates are derived from the Asian poppy seed and include Heroin, Methadone, Opium, Morphine, Codeine, and almost all prescription pain pills such as Oxys and Percocet.

40. Name three common opiates usually referred to by their medical name.

Vicodin, Percocet, Tylenol 3, and Methadone

41. How do opiates usually make users feel?
They they take away pain

42. What is heroin?
Heroin is a white powder usually wrapped in paper (known as a "wrap").

43. How is heroin prepared?
Is generally diluted with powdered glucose, although crooked drug dealers sometimes dilute or "cut" heroin with talcum powder or flour, which is highly dangerous for users. The powder mixes with water; the solution is then warmed and then injected intravenously. Heroin powder may also be snorted.

44. What is the main ingredient in heroin?
Morphine

45. In what common ways is heroin taken?
Snorted or injected

46. How does is make a user feel after they have taken the drug?
Shortly after the drug is snorted or injected, it produces an extreme feeling of ecstasy. Heroin works on the pleasure centers in the brain. The drug is taken for its euphoric and calming effects, which produces a warm, happy feeling.

47. What happens to a user after the drug wear off?
Nausea and vomiting frequently occurs after the drug wears off. Long-term continued use may include infection of the heart lining and valves, pulmonary complications, including various types of pneumonia. When someone tries to detoxify themselves from heroin, they will experience a series of withdrawal symptoms, including diarrhea, insomnia, and muscle aches. The withdrawal symptoms will start within a few hours after the person stops using heroin, with the peak occurring within 24-72 hours.

48. What are the long-term effects of herein?
Chronic users may develop collapsed veins, infection of the heart lining and valves, and liver disease.

49. Does a person develop a tolerance for heroin?
With physical dependence, the body has developed a tolerance and withdrawal symptoms may occur if use is reduced or stopped.

50. What is the best way for a user to detoxify from heroin?
Under the care of a physician

51. What is alcohol made from?

Alcohol is created when grains, fruits, or vegetables are fermented. Fermentation is a process that uses yeast or bacteria to change the sugars in the food into alcohol.

52. What does alcohol do to the body after it is taken?

Makes people feel relaxed and less anxious. Depending on the person, alcohol may make an individual seem extremely friendly, talkative, frisky, aggressive or angry.

53. Alcohol is very high in what? **Empty calories**

54. What does DUI stand for and what does it mean?
Driving under the influence (DUI)

55. What does DWI stand for and what does it mean?
Driving while intoxicated or (DWI).

56. What are the four parts to alcoholism?
        1.) cravings,
        2.) loss of control,
        3.) physical dependence,
        4.) tolerance.

57. What is a hangover?
    A "hang over" is what happens when the body enters alcohol withdrawal and headaches emerge, which are caused by extreme dehydration of the brain. The brain is literally being pulled away from the skull, leading to throbbing aches and sharp pains at attachment points like the temples and base of the neck.

58. What does being "present" mean?
    Being "present" means always being aware of what is going on in your life every minute.

59. What does drinking in moderation mean?
    Only occasionally and not having more than two drinks.

60. In what ways are you going to show responsibility when drinking? Answers may vary but may include:
        Do not drive if you are going to drink
        Only drink in moderation

61. What is counterfeit happiness? **Answers may vary**

62. What can you do to deal with your problems instead of drinking or using drugs?
    Answers may vary

63. Answers may vary

10
Buying Your First Home

Two Cents worth:

There is no feeling of achieving the American Dream than buying first home and sticking that key in the door.

Dr. Mia Y. Merritt

DATE _____

1. Explain why owning a home is more expensive than renting.

   _____

   _____

   _____

2. How far in advance should you begin saving in preparation for buying your home?

   _____

3. Name at least three things that you must do even before approaching an agent for a loan.

   I. _____

   II. _____

   III. _____

4. What is the purpose of a pre-qualification?

_____

_____

5. What is the first official step in the home-buying process?

_____

_____

6. Where can you go to get a mortgage loan?

_____

_____

7. What are some of the documents that you will need for the pre-approval process?

   I. _____

   II. _____

   III. _____

8. Why is good credit important when trying to buy a house?

_____

_____

9. What is the Good Faith Estimate and the purpose of it (GFE)?

_____

_____

10. Your mortgage payment should not be more than what percentage of your gross monthly income? _____ What is this called? _____

11. Your entire debt load should not be more than what percentage of your gross monthly income? _____ What is this called? _____

12. The amount of house that you can afford depends on what?

_____

_____

13. What does the word "term" mean?

_____

_____

14. Explain what a fixed rate is.

_____

_____

15. Explain what an ARM is?

_____

_____

16. What is the advantage of a fixed rate?

_____

_____

17. What is the disadvantage of a fixed rate?

_____

_____

18. What is the advantage of an ARM?

_____

19. What is the disadvantage of an ARM?

_____

_____

20. What are the benefits of a 15 year mortgage?

_____

_____

21. What is the drawback of a 15 year mortgage?

_____

_____

22. Name a reason why a person would choose an ARM?

_____

_____

23. Name a reason why a person would choose a fixed rate?

_____

_____

24. A loan that does not exceed 80% of the value of the property is called a what?

_____

_____

25. A loan that only requires 3.5% down as a payment is what kind of loan? _____

26. A loan that may not require anything down is called a what? _____

27. What are the four components of an ARM?

　　　i. _____

　　　ii. _____

　　　iii. _____

　　　iv. _____

28. In your own words, explain an interest-only mortgage.

_____

_____

29. If you have bad credit and do not qualify for a conventional loan, you can be a prime candidate for what kind of mortgage?

_____

30. Lenders who take advantage of the elderly and the economically deprived by influencing them to refinance or take out loans with high fees are called what kind of lenders?

_____

31. What does APR stand for and what is it?

_____

_____

_____

32. The Truth in Lending Law requires mortgage companies to do what for customers?

_____

_____

_____

33. The mortgage APR may come in two different types of forms: **Effective** APR or **Nominal** APR. Explain the difference between the two.

_____

_____

_____

34. Name at least five characteristics in predatory lending.

    I. _____

    II. _____

    III. _____

    IV. _____

    V. _____

35. What are discount points and what is the purpose of them?

_____

_____

_____

36. What are some things that you should take into consideration when house shopping?

    I. _____

    II. _____

    III. _____

37. Name five attributes that are important to you when purchasing a home.

I. _____

II. _____

III. _____

IV. _____

V. _____

38. What is the purpose of a Real-estate Agent?

_____

_____

_____

39. Who pays the commission to the Real-estate Agent? _____

40. What is the incentive for a Real-estate Agent when the price of the home you buy is high?

_____

_____

_____

41. How can a buyer benefit if there is no Real-estate Agent?

_____

_____

_____

42. Subprime mortgages are typically offered to people whose credit scores are below what? _____

43. What are the drawbacks of prepayment penalties?

_____

44. When you find a home that you like and you sign a contract, what is the next thing that you should do?

45. Explain what it means to go into Escrow.

46. What is the purpose of a Property Appraisal?

47. A Property Appraisal is for the _____ and a home inspection is for the _____.

48. In your own words, explain what happens on Closing Day.

49. Name at least three documents that you will receive on closing day.

I. _____

II. _____

III. _____

50. How does a homeowner get a tax break during tax time?

_____

_____

_____

In the space below draw a picture or cut out pictures of the kind of house that you would one day like to live in.

Time to Reflect

Buying a house can be a very exciting time, but also a very stressful one – especially when you are blindsided by all the additional costs involved. Explain how important buying your own home is to you. Describe your ideal home and how you will prepare for buying this home.

Self-check

- ✓ I will save at least one year in advance for my first home (if necessary).
- ✓ During this time, I will request and review my Credit Reports and seek to correct all errors or inaccuracies on them.
- ✓ I will pay off as many bills as possible, especially those with high balances.
- ✓ When ready, I will seek at least two mortgage estimates during the pre-approval process.
- ✓ I will compare the Good Faith Estimates of both lenders and choose the best rates and terms for me.
- ✓ I will choose the type of mortgage that is the best fit for me (conventional, FHA, Veterans, fixed or ARM).
- ✓ I will stay clear of subprime mortgages and predatory lenders.
- ✓ I will ask about any points I have to pay, and if so, how much those discount points will cost me (the more expensive the home, the more expensive the points).
- ✓ I will determine if I need a Real Estate Agent or if I will find a house for sale on my own.
- ✓ I will choose a neighborhood that is not in a flood zone, not high in crime, and is conducive to my needs.
- ✓ I will choose a home that I am at least 95% happy with.
- ✓ I will be sure to get a property appraisal and home inspection before closing the deal on the home.
- ✓ I will pay my mortgage on time until I am ready to purchase a bigger home or until my mortgage is paid in full!

Chapter 10 Answer Key

1. Explain why owning a home is more expensive than renting.
Because as a homeowner, you must pay for everything including repairs, utilities, landscaping, etc.

2. How far in advance should you begin saving in preparation for buying your home?
At least a minimum in advance in order to save the amount of money you need.

3. Name at least three things that you must do even before approaching an agent for a loan.

    ✓ **Save money for the down payment and all upfront costs.**
    ✓ **Pay as many of your bills off as possible, especially the ones with high balances.**
    ✓ **Review your Credit Report and correct any errors on it.**

4. What is the purpose of a pre-qualification?
It helps you focus on homes you can afford. A prequalification is when a professional gives you an estimate of how much money you "may" be able to borrow based upon your gross income and amount of debt.

5. What is the first official step in the home-buying process?
Getting a pre-approval

6. Where can you go to get a mortgage loan?
Different financial institutions give mortgage loans, such as credit unions, banks, pension funds, insurance companies and finance companies.

7. What are some of the documents that you will need for the pre-approval process?

    ✓ **Your last four paycheck stubs**
    ✓ **Six months worth of bank statements from all bank accounts you have**
    ✓ **Three years worth of tax returns**
    ✓ **Proof of any additional income**
    ✓ **Proof of how you will make the down payment**
    ✓ **Written explanations for any late payments you may have on your Credit Report**
    ✓ **Written explanations for any charge offs, repossessions, evictions or other derogatory entries on your credit report.**

8. Why is good credit important when trying to buy a house?

The better your credit is, the better interest rate you will be offered, which will save hundreds of thousands of dollars down the line.

9. What is the Good Faith Estimate and the purpose of it (GFE)?

An estimate and must be provided within three business days of applying for a loan. It is a standard form which is intended to be used to compare different offers from different lenders or brokers. It includes an itemized list of fees and costs associated with your loan estimate. It must be provided to a customer by a mortgage lender or broker in the United States. This is required by the Real Estate Settlement Procedures Act (RESPA).

10. Your mortgage payment should not be more than what percentage of your gross monthly income? _____ What is this called?

Your mortgage payment should not be more than 32% of your gross monthly income. This figure is known as your Gross Debt Service (GDS) **ratio.**

11. Your entire monthly income should not be more than what percentage of your gross monthly income? _____ What is this called?

Your entire monthly debt load should not be more than 40% of your gross monthly income. This figure is called your Total Debt Service (TDS) ratio.

12. The amount of house that you can afford depends on what?

The amount of house you can afford to buy depends on the terms of your mortgage and the interest rate.

13. What does the word "term" mean?

The term is the total length of time over which payments will be paid. This is normally 15 or 30 years.

14. Explain what a fixed rate is.

This is a mortgage in which the interest rate does not change during the entire life of the loan. Most fixed-rate loans are amortized for a certain period of time, meaning if the borrower makes the principal and interest payment every month over the term as agreed, the loan will be paid in full at the end of that time.

15. Explain what an ARM is?

An Adjustable Rate Mortgage (ARM) has an interest rate that is fixed for the first several years of the loan (typically 3, 5, or 7 years) then goes up or down for the remainder of the loan based on market conditions.

16. What is the advantage of a fixed rate?

If you take out a fixed rate loan when rates are low, the fixed rate would enable you to lock in the low rates and not be concerned with fluctuations as in an ARM.

17. What is the disadvantage of a fixed rate?

If the market interest rates decline, you are stuck with paying a higher interest rate.

18. What is the advantage of an ARM?
The interest rate in the early years of an ARM is usually much lower than that of a conventional fixed rate 30 year mortgage, which makes an ARM more affordable for people whose incomes are lower now than they expect it to be in a few years.

19. What is the disadvantage of an ARM?
Your monthly payment increases every month and can triple or quadruple what you start out paying.

20. What are the benefits of a 15 year mortgage?
A 15-year term lowers your interest rate, reduces total interest payments, and increases principal payments.

21. What is the drawback of a 15 year mortgage?
It also increases your monthly payment.

22. Name a reason why a person would choose an ARM?
A person would choose an ARM if they plan on moving within five years and won't be in the house when and if the market rates rise.

A person may also choose an ARM if the rates are very low at the time they buy their house and they would benefit.

A person may also choose an arm if they do not have the money to pay a high monthly mortgage payment, but anticipate having a higher income in the next few years and will be able to afford the payment when it rises.

23. Name a reason why a person would choose a fixed rate?
A person would choose a fixed rate so that they won't have to worry about their mortgage payment rising with market trends. A person would also choose a fixed rate if rates are down and they will be able to lock in the rate they get.

24. A loan that does not exceed 80% of the value of the property is called a what?
A standard loan is a loan that does not exceed 80% of the lending value of the property and is either fixed or adjustable.

25. A loan that only requires 3.5% down as a payment is what kind of loan?
An FHA Loan

26. A loan that may not require anything down is called a what?
A Veteran's Loan

27. What are the four components of an ARM?
(1) an index, (2) a margin, (3) an interest rate cap structure, and (4) an initial interest rate period.

28. In your own words, explain what an interest –only mortgage.

Answers may vary, but may include:
payments are made up of interest only and do not include any principal.

29. If you have bad credit and do not qualify for a conventional loan, you can be a prime candidate for what kind of mortgage?
A subprime mortgage

30. Lenders who take advantage of the elderly and the economically deprived and influences them to refinance or take out loans with high fees are called what?
Predatory Lenders

31. What does APR stand for and what is it?
APR stands for Annual Percentage Rate and has to do with how much money you will be paying upfront in order to get the best rate for your loan.

32. The Truth in Lending Law requires mortgage companies to do what for customers?
The *Federal Truth in Lending Law* requires mortgage companies to list the APR of their loans when they advertise an interest rate.

33. The mortgage APR may come in two different types of forms: Effective APR or Nominal APR. Explain the difference between the two.
An *Effective APR* looks at the simple interest generated in one year. The *Nominal APR* evaluates compound interest in one year and is more accurate.

34. Name at least five characteristics in predatory lending.
   - ✓ **Excessive Fees:**
   - ✓ **Prepayment Penalty:**
   - ✓ **Tax Refund Anticipation Loans (RALs):**
   - ✓ **Insurance and Other Unnecessary Products:**
   - ✓ **Abusive and Abnormal Prepayment Penalties:**
   - ✓ **Loan Flipping:**
   - ✓ **Mandatory Arbitration:**

35. What are discount points and what is the purpose of them?
Discount points are additional, up-front fees, paid in lieu of higher interest rates. When your money is scarce, lenders routinely charge points, also known as Loan Origination Fees. Each "point" is equal to 1 percent of the loan amount.

36. What are some things that you should take into consideration when house shopping?
Answers may vary, but may include:
   - ✓ **Find the neighborhood or development that you would like to live in.**
   - ✓ **Crime rates, gated communities, transportation, and closeness to family and friends may be things to consider.**
   - ✓ **You would also need to be sure that you are not buying a home that is in a flood zone.**
   - ✓ **How many bedrooms and bathrooms would you like?**
   - ✓ **Do you want a one or two story home?**

- ✓ Would you prefer a town home or condominium?
- ✓ A gated community or open neighborhood?
- ✓ Do you want a pool?
- ✓ An office? A family room? A garage?

37. Name five attributes that are important to you when purchasing a home.
Answers will vary

38. What is the purpose of a Real-estate Agent?
Your Real Estate Agent's job is to provide you with pertinent information about homes for sale and take you out to look at homes.

39. Who pays the commission to the Real-estate Agent?
The seller

40. What is the incentive for a Real-estate Agent when the price of the home you buy is high?
The more the cost of the house, the higher the real-estate commission.

41. How can a buyer benefit if there is no Real-estate Agent?
When there is no realtor, there is greater opportunity of talking the price of the house down because the seller does not have that 3% commission to pay to the realtor, so if the asking price of the house is $230,000, you have a 3% window of negotiation.

42. Subprime mortgages are typically offered to people whose credit scores are below what? **Below 600**

43. What are the drawbacks of prepayment penalties?
Over the next few years the borrowers may manage to improve their credit and want to obtain a new mortgage that has lower interest and lower payments. However, the prepayment penalty on the original mortgage (which often equals 5% of the original loan) is so high that it eats up any equity the homeowners have built up and can even leave them owing more money. Homeowners often are trapped into keeping the original, high-interest mortgage.

44. When you find a home that you like and you sign a contract, what is the next thing that you should do? **Get a home inspection**

45. Explain what it means to go into Escrow.
The money and/or documents in the Escrow Account are released when all terms of the agreement are met. The rationale behind having this account is to protect the lender by ensuring that you pay your taxes and insurance on time.

46. What is the purpose of a Property Appraisal?
To make sure that you are not overpaying for the house.

47. A Property Appraisal is for the _____ and a home inspection is for the _____. **Lender, buyer**

48. In your own words, explain what happens on Closing Day.
This is the big day, the day that the house officially becomes yours! To close, means to "close" the deal on the contract made to buy the home. At closing, the transfer of ownership of the house from the seller to you will officially be made and all monies owed will be paid during this time. You will be asked to sign many documents and affidavits during closing. Joining you around the table at this Closing Meeting will typically be you, the seller, possibly an attorney, your Real Estate Agent (if used), and the Closing Agent. Your lender may also attend. It is the Closing Agent who will conduct the meeting. On the day of closing, you must present the Homeowner's Insurance Policy. The seller will present proof that specified repairs were made (if applicable), bring warranties and/or other relevant documents pertaining to the home. Other documents specific to the transaction may also be brought.

49. Name at least three documents that you will receive on closing day.
Answers may vary, but may include:
- **Mortgage Note:**
- **Title or Deed:**
- **Truth-in-Lending Statement:**
- **Settlement Statement:**
- **Certificate of Occupancy:**

50. How does a homeowner get a tax break during tax time?
As long as your mortgage balance is smaller than the price of your home, the interest you pay is fully deductible on your tax return unless the home is more than one million dollars. If you are the proud owner of a multimillion-dollar mansion, the Internal Revenue Service (IRS) will limit your deductible interest. Interest is the largest component of your mortgage payment and offers you a huge tax break when you file your taxes.

11

All About the Military

Two Cents worth:

Marriage is like the army. Everybody complains, but you'd be surprised at how many re-enlist.

Anonymous

DATE _____

1. On the lines below, write three things that you know about the military.

   I. _____

   II. _____

   III. _____

2. Are you considering going into the military? ___ yes ___ no

3. Why or why not?

_____

_____

_____

4. If your answer is **yes**, write down the branch that you have decided to join and the reason why you chose that particular branch.

   Branch: _____

_____

_____

If you have no desire to go into the military, try and answer as many questions as you can from the book. It's good to be knowledgeable of different things.

5. Name the five branches of the military.

   I. _____

   II. _____

   III. _____

   IV. _____

   V. _____

6. Name at least two facts about each military branch.

ARMY:

   I. _____

   II. _____

NAVY:

   I. _____

   II. _____

AIRFORCE:

   I. _____

   II. _____

MARINES:

   I. _____

   II. _____

COAST GUARD:

   I. _____

   II. _____

7. Why is it important to do well on the ASVAB?

_____

_____

_____

8. What is the purpose of having the Armed Forces Reserves?

_____

_____

_____

9. Which two branches of the military has a National Guard?

_____ & _____

10. What are the two smallest branches in the military?

_____ & _____

11. Which branch of the military maintains "freedom of the seas" when the national interest requires it? _____

12. Which branch defends the United States and its interests through utilization of air and space? _____

13. Which branch organizes and trains soldiers for land warfare?
_____

14. Which branch enforces the law through boating safety, sea rescue, and illegal immigration? _____

15. Which branch protects and defends the US by way of ground troops, armor tanks, artillery, attack helicopters, tactical nuclear weapons, etc?
_____

16. Which branch is responsible for all military satellites, and controls all of the Nation's strategic nuclear ballistic missiles? _____

17. Which branch is nicknamed, *"The Infantry of the Navy"*? _____

18. What is the biggest difference between the Reserves and the National Guard?

_____

_____

_____

ORGANIZATIONAL STRUCTURE

19. Who heads the Department of Defense? _____

20. Who appoints the head of the Department of Defense? _____

21. How many military departments are there? _____ Name them.

_____

_____

_____

22. What is the title of the person who heads the military departments?

_____

23. What is the title of the person who heads the Army?

_____

24. What is the title of the person who heads the Navy?

_____

25. What is the title of the person who heads the Air Force?

_____

26. What is the title of the person who heads the Marines?

_____

27. What are the two type of background checks that the military conducts on each applicant?

_____ & _____

28. The four flag officers mentioned above are made up of a group called what?

_____

29. Which branch of the military does not fall under the Department of Defense?

_____

30. Which department does the above branch fall under?

_____

31. What are the penalties for telling a lie (or lies) to get into the military and then getting caught after enlistment?

_____

_____

_____

32. What is the purpose of basic training?

_____

_____

_____

33. What are the two types of strength that basic training teaches?

_____ & _____

34. What are the (2) titles of the individuals who will be over you in basic training?

_____ & _____

35. Which branch of the military does not mix men and women in basic training?

    _____

36. What does AWOL stand for?

    _____

37. What does AWOL mean?

    _____

    _____

    _____

38. What can be a penalty of going AWOL and getting caught?

    _____

    _____

    _____

39. What is the difference between going AWOL 30 days or less v/s more than 30 days or more?

    _____

    _____

40. What is the GI (Government Issued) bill?

    _____

    _____

41. When does a soldier decide whether they want to participate in the GI bill.?

    _____

42. Can a soldier change his or her mind about participating in the G.I. bill later on down the line? _____

43. When can a soldier receive a retirement of up to 50% of their base military pay?

_____

_____

44. What is the percentage of retirement you get after 30 years of service?

_____

45. What are some of the benefits of joining the military?

        i. _____

       ii. _____

      iii. _____

TRUE/FALSE

46. Everyone who joins the military automatically gets the GI Bill benefits. _____

47. Each of the armed forces has a National Guard. _____

48. The National Guard is owned by the US Government. _____

49. Your low score from ASVAB Test limits the jobs that you can choose from in the military. _____

50. You must sign up for at least two years in the military. _____

Time to Reflect

As has been said, the military is not for everyone, but for those who decide to join, it can be very rewarding. Talk about your thoughts on joining the military. Have you ever considered it? Why or why not? What kinds of things have you heard? Talk about what you learned about the military as a result of reading the book and other thought you may have.

Self-check
- Before joining the military, I will be absolutely sure that this is want I want to do.
- I will research each branch and choose the one that is the best fit for me.
- I will take practice tests and do the best I can on the ASVAB.
- I will prepare myself physically for Basic Training.
- I will sign up for the Educational Benefits while in Basic Training (I knowing that this is a one-time decision and I can not change my mind).
- I will do the best that I can to serve my country while in the military.
- I will save as much money as I can and use my money wisely while serving in the Armed Forces.
- I will make my country and myself proud as a member of the US military!

Chapter 11 Answer Key

Answers will vary for questions 1-4.

5. Name the five branches of the military.
>   **ARMY**
>   **NAVY**
>   **AIRFORCE**
>   **MARINE CORPS**
>   **COAST GUARD**

6. Name at least two facts about each military branch.
Answers will vary

7. Why is it important to do well on the ASVAB?
Answers will vary, but may include:
Because the score that you get on this test will determine the type of job you will train for in the military. The higher your scores are, the better your chances are of selecting from a wider variety of jobs.

8. What is the purpose of having Armed Forces Reserves?
The primary purpose of the Reserves and National Guard is to provide a reserve force to supplement the active duty forces when needed.

9. Which two branches of the military has a National Guard?
Army and Air force

10. What are the two smallest branches in the military?
The Marines and Coastguard

11. Which branch of the military maintains "freedom of the seas" when the national interest requires it? **Navy**

12. Which branch defends the United States and its interests through utilization of air and space? **Airforce**

13. Which branch organizes and trains soldiers for land warfare? **Army**

14. Which branch enforces the law through boating safety, sea rescue, and illegal immigration? **Coastguard**

15. Which branch protects and defends the US by way of ground troops, armor tanks, artillery, attack helicopters, tactical nuclear weapons, etc? **Army**

16. Which branch is responsible for all military satellites, and controls all of the Nation's

strategic nuclear ballistic missiles? **Airforce**

17. Which branch is nicknamed, "*The Infantry of the Navy*"? **Marines**

18. What is the biggest difference between the Reserves and the National Guard?
The biggest difference between the Reserves and the National Guard is that the Reserves belong to the Federal Government, while the National Guard belongs to the individual state's government.

19. Who heads the Department of Defense?
The Secretary of Defense

20. Who appoints the head of the Department of Defense?
The President of the United States.

21. How many military departments are there? _____ Name them.
Three: the Secretary of the Army, the Secretary of the Air Force, and the Secretary of the Navy.

22. What is the title of the person who heads the military departments?
The Secretary of Defense

23. What is the title of the person who heads the Army?
The Army is commanded by a four-star general, known as the *Army Chief of Staff*

24. What is the title of the person who heads the Navy?
The Navy is commanded by a four-star admiral, called the *Chief of Naval Operations*

25. What is the title of the person who heads the Air Force?
The top military member in the Air Force is the *Air Force Chief of Staff*

26. What is the title of the person who heads the Marines?
The Marines are commanded by a four-star general called the *Commandant of the Marine Corps*

27. What are the two type of background checks that the military conducts on each applicant?
Credit and Criminal

28. The four flag officers mentioned above are made up of a group called what?
These four Flag Officers make up a group called the *Joint Chiefs of Staff (JSC).*

29. Which branch of the military does not fall under the Department of Defense?
Coast Guard does not fall under the Department of Defense.

30. Which department does the above branch fall under?
Department of Homeland Security

Dr. Mia Y. Merritt, M&M Motivating
Life After High School: Valuable Life Skills for the Goal-Oriented Achiever!

31. What are the penalties for telling a lie (or lies) to get into the military and then getting caught after enlistment?
This offense is punishable by a $10,000 fine and/or three years in prison! If you get away with it long enough to actually enlist, and are caught later, it becomes a military offense and you can be prosecuted for a violation of *Article 83* of the *Uniform Code of Military Justice (UCMJ)*, which states:

"Any person who--
1. procures his own enlistment or appointment in the armed forces by
knowingly false representation or deliberate concealment as to his qualifications for that enlistment or appointment and receives pay or allowances thereunder; or

2. procures his own separation from the armed forces by knowingly false
representation or deliberate concealment as to his eligibility for that separation; shall be punished as a court-martial may direct."

The *Manual for Courts Martial* (MCM) lists the maximum punishment for a violation of this article as: dishonorable discharge, reduction to the lowest enlisted rank, forfeiture of all pay and allowances, and confinement at hard labor for two years. The Enlistment Contract, which is (DD Form 4/1) can not make this any more plain. Paragraph 13a of the contract signed by the recruit states:

13a. My acceptance for enlistment is based on the information I have given in my application for enlistment. If any of that information is false or incorrect, this enlistment may be voided or terminated administratively by the Government, or I may be tried by Federal, civilian, or military court, and, if found guilty, may be punished.

32. What is the purpose of basic training?
To teach war-fighting skills.

33. What are the two types of strength that basic training teaches?
Mental and physical

34. What are the (2) titles of the individuals who will be over you in basic training?
Training Instructors (T.I.'s) and Drill Instructors (D.I.'s)

35. Which branch of the military does not mix men and women in basic training?
Marine Corps

36. What does AWOL stand for?
***"Absent Without Leave"* (AWOL)**

37. What does AWOL mean?
AWOL means that a soldier runs away from the military to return to civilian life.

38. What can be a penalty of going AWOL and getting caught?
If a soldier goes AWOL while at basic training, he or she is subject to the same charges and punishments as soldiers who are part of regular units. Going AWOL is

covered under Article 86 of the *Uniform Code of Military Justice*, which states that if a soldier:

> *"absents himself or remains absent from his unit, organization, or place of duty at which he is required to be at the time prescribed," he or she "shall be punished as a court-martial may direct."*

39. What is the difference between going AWOL 30 days or less v/s more than 30 days or more?
Out-processing at Fort Sill occurs if the soldier has been dropped from the rolls of a basic-training unit, which happens after 30 days of being declared AWOL. Many people advise AWOL recruits to wait 30 days before turning themselves in if they really want to leave the Military.

40. In your own words, what is the Government Issued (GI) bill?
Answers will vary

41. When does a soldier decide whether they want to participate in the GI bill.?
During Basic Training and this is the only time.

42. Can a soldier change his or her mind about participating in the G.I. bill later on down the line? **No. A soldier can not change his or her mind later on.**

43. When can a soldier receive a retirement of up to 50% of their base military pay?
After they have served 20 years in the Armed Forces

44. What is the percentage of retirement you get after 30 years of service? **75% of your salary**

45. What are some of the benefits of joining the military?
Answers will vary, but may include:

- **Traveling the world**
- **College and medical benefits**
- **Free room and board**

46. Everyone who joins the military automatically gets the GI Bill benefits. **FALSE**
47. Each of the armed forces has a National Guard. **FALSE**
48. The National Guard is owned by the US Government. **FALSE**
49. Your low score from ASVAB Test limits the jobs that you can choose from in the military. **TRUE**
50. You must sign up for at least two years in the military. **TRUE**

Other Books by Dr. Mia Y. Merritt
1-866-560-7652

Go to www.miamerritt.com to order

Destined for Great Things (Book)

Destined for Great Things (Workbook)

Prosperity is Your Birthright (Book)

Prosperity is Your Birthright (Workbook)

Words of Inspiration: Golden Nuggets for the Wise at Heart

The Road to Inner Joy and Peace

Life After High School: Valuable Life Skills for the Goal-oriented Achiever!

Dr. Mia Y. Merritt
www.miamerritt.com

M&M Motivating
President/CEO
Dr. Mia Y. Merritt
1-866-560-7652

Other books written
by Mia Merritt:

Destined for Great Things!
Destined for Great Things Workbook
Prosperity is Your Birthright!
Prosperity is Your Birthright Workbook
Prosperity is Your Birthright Journal
Words of Inspiration:
Golden Nuggets for the Wise at Heart
Life After High School

Dr. Mia Y. Merritt

Graduation Ceremony Keynote Speaker
Conference Retreat Speaker
Women's Conference Speaker
Youth Motivator
Workshop Facilitator
Teen/Youth Trainer
Seminar Conductor
Personal Life Coach

For booking information, call
1-866-560-7652
or visit us at

www.miamerritt.com

www.ingramcontent.com/pod-product-compliance
Lightning Source LLC
Chambersburg PA
CBHW081351160426
43198CB00015B/2584